P9-CAM-879

BOOK A
READING FOR CONCEPTS

"We learn to read in order to read to learn."

WILLIAM LIDDLE

General Editor
Director, Instructional Services
Colorado Springs Public Schools
Director of the Reading Clinic, the Colorado College
Colorado Springs, Colorado

BOOK A READING

FOR CONCEPTS

Second Edition

WEBSTER DIVISION
McGRAW-HILL BOOK COMPANY

New York   St. Louis   San Francisco
Aukland   Bogotá   Düsseldorf   Johannesburg   London   Madrid
Mexico   Montreal   New Delhi   Panama   Paris   São Paulo
Singapore   Sydney   Tokyo   Toronto

Contributing Authors for the Reading for Concepts Series:

Linda Barton, feature writer for *St. Louis Today.*

Roberta H. Berry, elementary school teacher, writer.

Barbara Broeking, journalist and educational publications editor.

Eth Clifford, author of many volumes of fiction and poetry for youth.

Ellen Dolan, juvenile book author.

Barbara R. Frey, Professor of Education, State University College, Buffalo, N.Y.

Ruth Harley, author and editor of young people's periodicals.

Phyllis W. Kirk, children's book editor.

Richard Kirk, author of science, social studies, and reading books for youth.

Thomas D. Mantel, attorney and juvenile author.

Marilyn F. Peachin, journalist and editor.

James N. Rogers, author-editor of science and social studies resource books.

James J. Pflaum, author and editor of current events periodicals.

Gloria S. Rosenzweig, writer of primary teaching materials.

Jean Shirley, author of juvenile books.

Rosemary Winebrenner, editor of children's books.

Jean White, journalist and writer of young people's reference materials.

Educational Consultant:

Dr. Ruth Gallant, The Center for Teaching and Learning, University of North Dakota, Grand Forks, N.D.

Statisticians for Original Prepublication Field Trials:

Dr. Michael Grady and Dr. Roslyn Grady, Colorado Springs, Colo.

Robert Hampson, Pupil Accounting and Testing Services, Colorado Springs, Colo.

Resource Committee:

Ruth Liddle, Eleanor Wier, Ruth Mitchell, Jean Keeley, and Joseph Tockman.

Project Editor: Carol Washburne
Designer: Jim Darby
Editing Supervisor: Sal Allocco
Production Supervisor: Karen Romano

Illustrators: James Cummings; Portia Takajian, GAI
Cover Photo: George Hall/Woodfin Camp

Copyright © 1977, 1970 McGraw-Hill, Inc. All Rights Reserved. Printed in the United States of America. No part of this publication may be reproduced, stored in a retrieval system, or transmitted, in any form or by any means, electronic, mechanical, photocopying, recording, or otherwise, without the prior written permission of the publisher.

ISBN 0-07-037661-1

TABLE OF CONTENTS

Notes to the Teacher   7/10

Concept I: *Change Is a Part of Life*   13

The Earl Was Busy   14

Do You Ever Wear a Mask?   16

Trash or Treasures   18

A Sky Full of Fish   20

Ladders or Steps   22

The Indians Who Breathe Thin Air   24

The Squirrel and the Acorn   26

Pet from the Stone Age   28

A Horse No Bigger Than a Cat   30

The Smallest Bird   32

Room to Grow   34

The Frog That Changes Color   36

Let's Trade   38

A Thread 100 Miles Long   40

When Jaws Can't Bite   42

Walking, Talking Ads   44

Can You Vote?   46

The Hat That Talked   48

The Tree That Was Always Different   50–53

The Rain Dance   54

The Leaf That Tells a Story   56

The Fish on the Mountain   58

A River of Ice   60

The River That Dug a Canyon   62

Volcano in a Field   64

How Cities Began   66

A Bag of Bugs   68

Are You a Little Doll?   70

Please Pass the Pepper   72

Send a Message   74

When Schools Were Different   76

Changing Lines   78

A Stone for a Sheep   80

The Year the Barn Burned Down   82

The Time of the Falling Leaves   84

Look for a Sign   86

A Leg Walking Right   88

How the Rabbit Got Its Shape   90–92

Concept II: *Some Changes Are Fast,*
Some Changes Are Slow 93

The New Fur Suit 94

Land of the Reindeer 96

Animal Skin Ball 98

The School on Wheels 100

Signs in the Desert 102

Kings and Queens of Candy 104

The Cat and the Clover 106

The Purple Martin Day 108

Before There Were Birds 110

Learning from Chimps 112

Plants That Cure 114

Does Your Skin Fit? 116

The Fight 118

Bells on Your Ears 120

Stone Money, Feather Money 122

The City That a Secret Built 124

Stop for Fair Rules 126

Old Job or New Job? 128

The Dog Who Could Not
Understand 130–133

The Moving Hill 134

The Day the Houses Fell Down 136

The River in the Ocean 138

Hurakan, God of the
Big Wind 140

Shapes from the Past 142

Rivers at Work 144

Ghost Town 146

The Pike Across the
Road 148

The Peach Basket Game 150

Whales in Trouble 152

The Big Dogs 154

Books in Chains 156

Sixteen Left Feet 158

Make a Fist 160

Something for Nothing 162

The Machine That Knows
the Answers 164

The Rope Stretchers 166

A Dusty Way to Count 168

Charts for Record Keeping 170–172

List of Difficult Words
by Story 173–176

Purpose

This book is one of eight in the series, "Reading for Concepts." It was designed to provide an opportunity for young readers to grow in reading experience while exploring a wide variety of ideas contained in several of the academic disciplines.

Two basic underlying concepts are reflected in this book. They are: *Change is a part of life*, and *Some changes happen faster than others*. The overriding concept in this book is the fact of change as a part of our lives.

To illustrate these concepts, stories have been written around intriguing pieces of information which reflect these ideas. The content has been drawn from the six disciplines of history, biology, economics, anthropology, mathematics, and geography. In this way a wide array of content for meeting various interests has been assured.

Six stories are presented in each discipline. A narrative follows after stories 18, 36, and 54. The narratives, largely drawn from folk literature, will provide a change of pace and are "just for fun" types of stories.

Teaching Procedure

The child will be given a diagnostic test at the beginning of the program to help the teacher in determining at which reading level he or she should be placed.

1. Discuss the title and picture clue in the story and establish purposes for reading it.

2. Present difficult words in advance. (There is an index at the back of this book which will direct the teacher in selecting the words expected to cause difficulties at each reading level.)

3. Have students read the story silently. A timed approach may be useful. The stories are all approximately 150 words long. Narratives lengths are listed. Begin with a reading time suitable to the average needs of the group. Moderate speed in reading is an indication of reading proficiency, but it is not the basic province of this series. As comprehension increases, the emphasis may switch to reducing reading time. At this time, use a stopwatch and figure each reader's rate for a story and encourage the pupil to read more quickly each subsequent time. By using the charts pupils can see their own progress.

4. Following each regular story is a test which is especially designed to improve specific skills in reading. There are charts at the end of this book on which to record scores of each skill tested. By carefully using these charts, teacher and pupil can make a diagnosis of specific skill weaknesses and also keep track of progress in each aspect of reading skill.

The sample exercise that begins the pupil's text should be reviewed carefully with all pupils. Each test item in the sample should be examined. Pupils should understand in advance exactly how they are to arrive at correct answers, whether they are expected to retain information, to verify from the text, to find the exact word needed, or to conjecture on the basis of information given. Success is necessary. The sample exercise will be found at the end of this discussion.

The skills tested in Book A are typical of those suggested in Bloom's Taxonomy of Educational Objectives. Bloom's Taxonomy is a way of ordering thinking from recall, the simplest thought process, to the most abstract order of thinking, synthesis. A taxonomy is a scale, the use of which is a means of establishing where along a hierarchy of thinking one is operating. The point of the test questions is to build a series of test items that incorporate the range of thinking skills as they are reflected in the Taxonomy.

Item 1. Knowledge of specific facts. The answers here must be selected from a group of possibilities. The correct answer selected from multiple alternatives is a directly stated fact in the story. This retention skill would correspond to Bloom's knowledge category, especially to "Knowledge of Specific Facts." The nature of the articles, of course, contributes to the awareness of some key facts about particular cultures, etc.

Item 2. Recognition of meaning of word in context. The student must choose and write the correct response. This skill corresponds to Bloom's "Knowledge of Terminology," especially to the area of "Familiarity with a large number of words in their common range of meaning."

Item 3. Competence with structural skills—finding an antecedent. This item is intended to make pupils aware of correct form and usage. An antecedent is defined as a word, phrase, or clause to which a pronoun refers. It will refer to an earlier occurrence, a person, or place. This skill falls within Bloom's "Knowledge of Conventions."

Item 4. Recognition of implications or inferences. This item requires selecting the correct inference from several choices. The response required comes from a multiple choice of implied details. The skill relates to Bloom's "Extrapolation."

Item 5. Ability to make substantiation from content. This item requires the reader to reread to prove a point. The reader must select the exact statement in the story which will match the test item word for word. This skill is specifically one of attention to the task of reading.

Item 6. Recognition of the meaning of the whole. This item requires the reader to select the answer which best describes the central theme of the story. This skill corresponds to Bloom's "Meaning of the Whole—Interpretation."

Item 7. Understanding of the meaning of words in context. This second vocabulary item stresses recognition of antonyms. The skill falls within Bloom's "Knowledge of Terminology." It is generally believed that if a person can give the opposite of a word there is understanding of the total concept on the continuum. This is frequently tested for in IQ and language development tests. This type of item is also helpful in developing reference skills.

Method

Each story has been written to the specifications for a controlled vocabulary and readability level. The readability level of this book was determined through application of the Spache Readability Formula for predicting vocabulary, and is appropriate for the beginning reader. See the manual for statistical information.

Words not in the controlled vocabulary list were limited to words according to standard lists of words suitable for pupils slightly older than their reading level would imply. In some cases, the content required the use of a highly specialized word. Such words are carefully defined by context clues in the story itself and are listed in the index.

Field Testing

In the testing population, a wide range of background and abilities of pupils were represented. See the manual for details. The results of extensive field testing were used to revise the materials until an optimum ease index was achieved. The testing suggests that finding the antecedent of a pronoun is very difficult for many children. Preliminary practice will be necessary as well as considerable support until a working understanding takes hold. See teaching notes with the sample selection for specific directions necessary to make the vital Question 3 a learning experience.

The teacher should also remind the reader where it is necessary to look back into the story to find answers.

Concept Recapitulations

After pupils have completed the text, the following suggestions may be helpful in conducting a discussion which will tie together the information carried in the individual articles in terms of the overall concept. This type of activity is important not for the particular information pupils will meet in these books but for the beginnings of building a wider view of the human environment. Information from widely divergent fields can interact to contribute to broad, intellectual awareness, whereas most education tends to fracture rather than serve the development of such wide-angle perspective.

Often, those youngsters most resistant to formal educational processing have drawn their own conclusions about the world and how it works. These students, in particular, may take fresh challenge from the experience of using pieces of information as the flexible building blocks for at least one unified meaningful whole. This type of reading is helping them practice the necessary modern skill of "continuous translation." Here skill building in reading has been attached not only to immediate short-range motivation and information accumulation but also to long-range creative reassessment of apparently dissimilar content. Great openness and considerable flexibility will be required from teachers who will make the greatest use of this aspect of

9

this reading program. The possibilities for student growth and awakenings are enormous.

A procedure such as the following is suggested:

"You have read stories about two big ideas. The first idea was that *change is a part of life.* In the beginning of the book you were asked to keep certain questions in mind. Can you answer these questions now?" (Pupils meet guiding questions on page 13.)

1. How many ways did you find that changes take place?

2. Do people usually want to change?

3. Have any of these changes affected you?

4. Are changes usually for the good?

5. Do all things change?

"The second big idea that you read about was that *some changes are fast; some changes are slow.* Can you now answer the following questions?" (Guide questions are on page 93.)

1. Why do some things change fast and other things change slowly?

2. What kind of things change slowly?

3. What kind of things change fast?

4. How many things can you think of that cause changes to happen?

Have a few priming possibilities ready to suggest, or shape them out of the early offerings from the group. Sophisticated statements and a review of specifics are not to be expected. Look for signs of mental play and the movement of information from one setting to another. It is perfectly reasonable to conclude with unanswered questions for pupils to ponder in retrospect. However, it is important to give pupils the satisfaction of enthusiastic acceptance of their early attempts at this type of open-ended speculation.

STEPS FOR THE READER

A. Turn to page 14. Look at the picture. Read the title. Think about what the story will say.

B. Study the words for this page on the list beginning on page 173.

C. Read the story carefully.

D. Put your name and the title of the story on a sheet of paper. Number from one to seven. Begin the test on the page next to the story.

1. This question asks you to remember something the story has told you. Which of the four choices will make the sentence say what the story does? Choose that statement.

2. This question asks you to find the word in the story that means the same as the words in slanting type. When the question gives you a paragraph number, read that part again to be sure you have the right word.

3. This question asks you to find a word that is pointed out by a smaller word. Words like *he, they,* and *it* stand for words that have been written before. Read Question 3. Who was playing cards? The Earl. You can see that the word *He* means the *Earl.* There are clues to the right answer. Think about your answer. In some tests, like the first one, the question contains all of the words you will need. Sometimes, you will have to reread the given paragraph in the story to find the word.

4. This question wants you to think about the story. The answer is not in your book. Read the choices. Choose the sentence that is the very best guess you might make from the ideas you have read in the story.

5. This question requires much care. You must match the test sentence *word for word* with the one in the story. Does your choice begin like the one in the story? Are all the words in the same place?

6. This question asks you to choose a statement about the entire story. Don't select an idea that fits only one small part. Your answer should fit all of the story.

7. The question points out the place in your story where you will find the right word. You must find a word that is the opposite of the one in Question 7. Think about the meaning. For the first story, count the sentences from one to five in the first paragraph. Read the fifth sentence again. Write the word that is the opposite of *go*.

E. Check your work. The answers for the first test are given below. Your teacher may let you use the answer key for other tests. She may check your work for you.

F. Put the number correct at the top of your paper. Now go back and recheck the answers that were wrong. Do you see now how the correct answer was better? How can you get ready to do the next test better?

G. Turn to page 170. The directions tell you how to put your score onto a record chart. Your teacher will tell you if you may write in the book. If not, he or she will help you make a copy for your notebook.

Looking for the Big Idea
See the following page for big ideas to think about as you read.

Just for Fun
Your book has three longer stories that are just for fun. These stories, beginning on pages 50, 90, and 130, are from old folktales. There are no questions to answer.

Answers for Practice Test, page 15

1. c	2. sandwich	3. Earl	4. c
5. a	6. c	7. stop	

I

Change Is a Part of Life

In this section you will read about many things that change. You will read about these things in the areas of anthropology (the study of human development), biology (the science that studies how things grow), geography (the study of the features of the earth), history (the study of past), economics (the study of the making of goods to use), and arithmetic.

Keep these questions in mind when you are reading.

1. How many ways can I see that changes took place?

2. Did people want to change?

3. Have all the changes affected me?

4. Were the changes usually good?

5. Does everything change in the long run?

The Earl Was Busy

1   The Earl of Sandwich was busy. He was playing cards. He liked games. He played all day. He did not stop to eat. He played all night. He did not sleep.

2   At last the Earl was hungry. He did not want to take time for dinner.

3   "Bring me my meat," he said. "Put it between two pieces of bread."

4   The Earl ate his bread and meat. The meat did not get on his fingers. He kept on playing cards.

5   "That looks good," his friends thought. They put their meat between two pieces of bread, too. They liked the way it tasted. "What a wonderful way to eat," they said.

6   Other people liked this new way of eating, too. They wanted their bread and meat fixed the way the Earl of Sandwich had his. What did they ask for?

1. The Earl asked for
    a. eggs and milk.   c. meat between bread.
    b. cake.   d. apples

2. The word in the story that means *meat between slices of bread* is _____.

3. The story says, "The Earl of Sandwich was busy. *He* was playing cards." The word *he* means the _____.

4. Which of the following does this story lead you to believe?
    a. The Earl of Sandwich had no friends.
    b. The Earl of Sandwich was not a very smart man.
    c. The sandwich was named for an Earl of Sandwich.

5. Why could the Earl go on playing cards? (Which sentence is exactly like the one in your book?)
    a. The meat did not get on his fingers.
    b. The meat was all gone.
    c. The meat on his fingers helped him win.

6. The main idea of the whole story is
    a. that most people sleep all day.
    b. that the Earl never got hungry.
    c. why the first sandwich was made.

7. The opposite of *go* (in sentence five) is _____.

Do You Ever Wear A Mask?

1   People have been using masks for thousands of years. Masks have been used in many ways. Some tribes wore masks when they went to war. They thought the masks helped them win. Others thought that wearing animal masks would make them strong. Others thought the world was run by gods. They made masks for these gods. The people danced before the masks. The people hoped the dancing would keep the gods happy.

2   Have you ever seen pictures of totem poles? Totem poles can be masks, too. These masks are painted one above the other. Many American Indians thought gods lived in these masks. They believed the gods in the totem poles took care of the people.

3   Indian medicine men and medicine women had masks. With the masks on, these Indians thought they could make sick people well.

4   Today, doctors wear masks. What other people wear masks? Do you ever wear a mask?

1. Animal masks were supposed to make people
   a. beautiful.   c. kind.
   b. strong.   d. happy.

2. The word in the story that means *coverings that hide faces* is _____ .

3. The story says, "Some tribes wore masks when *they* went to war." The word *they* means _____ .

4. Which of the following does this story lead you to believe?
   a. We use masks in different ways today.
   b. You have to wear a mask when you take medicine.
   c. You can never wear a mask.

5. What do we know about totem poles? (Which sentence is exactly like the one in your book?)
   a. Totem poles are trees that fall down.
   b. Totem poles can be masks, too.
   c. Totem poles are poles on ships.

6. The main idea of the whole story is that
   a. masks have been used in many ways.
   b. totem poles make people sick.
   c. Indians do not like medicine.

7. The opposite of *lose* (in sentence four) is _____ .

Trash or Treasures

1   Trash collectors come down the street. They take away cans and papers. They take away broken toys. They take all the things we do not want.

2   Thousands of years ago, people had trash, too. They threw away old baskets and broken bowls. They threw away broken tools. Time went by. The trash was covered up.

3   Today, scientists dig to find these things. They look at the broken bowls and baskets. They look at the tools. They learn many things about the people of long ago.

4   Some of the old things are beautiful. We do not call them trash. We call them treasures. We save them and take care of them.

5   A thousand years from now, people may find our trash. They may see old cans and papers. They may find such things as broken clocks and old toys. Do you think our trash will become their treasure?

1. Long ago, people threw away
       a. old baskets.   c. books.
       b. dolls.   d. candy.

2. The word in the story that means *old, broken things no one wants*
   is _____.

3. The story says, "Trash collectors come down the street. *They* take away cans and papers." The word *they* means
   _____.

4. Which of the following does the story lead you to believe?
       a. Scientists want to know about people of long ago.
       b. All scientists wear white coats when they are working.
       c. The trash collector is a scientist.

5. Why do scientists look at the things they find? (Which sentence is exactly like the one in your book?)
       a. They learn how to throw many old things away.
       b. They learn how to look at tools no one wants.
       c. They learn many things about the people of long ago.

6. The main idea of the whole story is that
       a. baskets are good for holding trash.
       b. trash collectors take away all our good things.
       c. some things of long ago are treasures today.

7. The opposite of *new* (paragraph two, sentence two) is _____.

A Sky Full of Fish

1   The sky is full of fish and animals. The fish and animals are kites. It is Kite Day in the park.

2   Kites go far back in time. Once people believed kites could carry their thoughts to the gods. Many people flew kites over their houses at night. They thought this kept them safe from all bad things at night.

3   Kites are fun. But they also have been of great help to us. People have used kites to learn more about the weather. Kites have been used in building bridges. Heavy wire cables for bridges have been pulled across water with the use of kites.

4   Once a great American put a key on a kite. He wanted to know more about lightning. Do you know who he was?

1. Kites flying over the houses at night were to keep people
   - a. happy.
   - c. quiet.
   - b. safe.
   - d. at home.

2. The word in the story that means *heavy wires across bridges* is _____.

3. The story says, "Kites are fun. But *they* have also been of great help to us." The word *they* means _____.

4. Which of the following does this story lead you to believe?
   - a. Today we fly kites for fun.
   - b. Today we fly kites to keep bad things away.
   - c. Today we use kites to hold our keys.

5. How have kites been used? (Which sentence is exactly like the one in your book?)
   - a. People have used kites to learn more about outer space.
   - b. People have used kites to learn more about the weather.
   - c. People have used kites to learn more about how to fly.

6. The main idea of the whole story is that
   - a. kites have been used in many ways.
   - b. it is hard to build a bridge.
   - c. fish like to fly kites.

7. The opposite of *under* (paragraph two, sentence three) is _____.

Ladders or Steps

1   An Indian child is living in an adobe (ə dō′ bē) house. Adobe is another word for bricks. Long ago, Indians made the adobe by hand from earth. Then they dried the adobe in the sun.

2   The Indian girl's house sits on top of six other adobe houses. The girl climbs up to her house on ladders. The Indian girl lives in a pueblo (pü eb′ lō). A pueblo is something like an apartment house.

3   Another child lives in a big city. She lives in a tall building. Her building is made of bricks, too. But these bricks are not made by hand. Many bricks are baked at one time. Then they are brought to the city.

4   This child's home is on top of six other homes, too. She walks up stone steps to her house. She lives in an apartment house.

5   Do you use ladders or stone steps to get to your house?

1. The Indians made adobe bricks from
       a. rocks.   c. earth.
       b. grass.   d. straw.

2. The word in the story that means *an Indian apartment house* is _____ .

3. The story says, "Many bricks are baked at one time. Then *they* are brought to the city." The word *they* means _____ .

4. Which of the following does this story lead you to believe?
       a. People who live at the top cannot come down.
       b. Everybody has to live in a pueblo.
       c. There are different ways to get to the top.

5. How does an Indian child get into the pueblo? (Which sentence is exactly like the one in your book?)
       a. The girl climbs on ladders to the top of the hill.
       b. The girl climbs up to her house on ladders.
       c. The girl climbs a hill to her house.

6. The main idea of the whole story is that
       a. city children cannot climb ladders.
       b. the Indian and the city child both live in apartments.
       c. Indians sit on steps going up to their apartment houses.

7. The opposite of *down* (paragraph two, sentence two) is _____ .

The Indians Who
Breathe Thin Air

1   Air goes up for thousands of miles. The higher the air, the thinner it gets. Then air is hard to breathe.

2   People who go up into high mountains often get dizzy. Breathing the thin air makes them dizzy.

3   Airplanes fly more than 15,000 feet above the sea. The air is very thin. Are the pilots dizzy? No. They breathe oxygen from a tank.

4   In South America, Indians live far up on the mountains. Their homes are more than 15,000 feet above the sea. The air is thin. The Indians are not breathing oxygen from a tank. But they do not get dizzy. They have lived in these mountains all their lives. Their lungs have changed. They have become large. The large lungs help the Indians breathe the thin air.

5   Sometimes the Indians go down to the low country. People living down there feel fine. But the Indians feel sick.

1. People who go up high in the mountains often get
    a. sleepy.   c. hungry.
    b. tired.   d. dizzy.

2. The word in the story that means *something that holds oxygen*

    is _____.

3. The story says, "People who go up into the high mountains often get dizzy. Breathing the thin air makes *them* dizzy." The

    word *them* means _____.

4. Which of the following does this story lead you to believe?
    a. People get used to the air where they live.
    b. Air is found only in tanks.
    c. Breathing is hard for the mountain Indians.

5. How do larger lungs help the Indians? (Which sentence is exactly like the one in your book?)
    a. The large lungs help the Indians sleep better.
    b. The large lungs help the Indians fly well in airplanes.
    c. The large lungs help the Indians breathe the thin air.

6. The main idea of the whole story is that
    a. Indians like to fly over mountains.
    b. mountain Indians can breathe thin air.
    c. airplanes can fly high over mountains.

7. The opposite of *small* (paragraph four, sentence nine) is

    _____.

The Squirrel and the Acorn

1   An acorn is a seed. It holds food for a new plant. It holds life for a new plant. Oak trees grow from acorns.

2   In the fall, a squirrel ran across a yard. It ran to a big oak tree. It looked for acorns. When the squirrel found them, it hid the acorns in the ground.

3   In the winter, it dug up the acorns to eat. When spring came, one acorn was still in the ground. The spring rains made the acorn soft. The sun made the ground warm. The acorn began to grow. A root went down. A small white shoot pushed up.

4   The small white shoot pushed through the top of the ground. Two small leaves came out. They were oak leaves.

5   Another oak tree was growing. It would become a big tree some day. Its acorns would drop to the ground. Would another squirrel find them and plant another tree?

1. The squirrel dug up the acorns in
   a. spring.   c. summer.
   b. fall.   d. winter.

2. The word in the story that means *a plant beginning to push out of the ground* is _____.

3. The story says, "Another oak tree was growing. *It* would become a big tree some day." The word *it* means _____.

4. Which of the following does this story lead you to believe?
   a. Animals can spread seeds.
   b. Animals stop trees from growing.
   c. Many squirrels don't like acorns.

5. What happened to the acorn that was left in the ground? (Which sentence is exactly like the one in your book?)
   a. The acorn looked for the squirrel.
   b. The acorn began to die.
   c. The acorn began to grow.

6. The main idea of the whole story is that
   a. an oak tree grew from an acorn a squirrel planted.
   b. squirrels like to live and play in big trees.
   c. an oak tree cannot grow from an acorn.

7. The opposite of *hard* (paragraph three, sentence three) is

   _____.

Pet from the Stone Age

1 Dogs are our friends. They work for us. They hunt with us. They play with us. But once, all over the world, dogs were wild.

2 Dogs go back to the Stone Age. All dogs had the same ancestor. It is believed that this ancestor was much like a wolf. Other animals, like the fox, came from this ancestor, too.

3 Thousands of years ago, people began to tame the wild dogs. When the dogs were tame, they were trained. The strong dogs became working animals. They were trained to pull heavy loads. They learned to keep watch over sheep and other animals. Working dogs had other jobs, too.

4 Some dogs were not strong. But they could help hunters find game. Other dogs were best as pets.

5 At first, there were only a few kinds of dogs. Today, there are more than 100 kinds.

1. We believe the ancestor of the dog was much like the
   a. fox.   c. wolf.
   b. cow.   d. fish.

2. The word in the story that means *an animal far back in another animal's family* is _____.

3. The story says, "When the dogs were tame, *they* were trained." The word *they* means _____.

4. Which of the following does this story lead you to believe?
   a. Animals never change.
   b. Most cats are just like dogs.
   c. People have helped change animals.

5. What happened to some strong dogs? (Which sentence is exactly like the one in your book?)
   a. The strong dogs turned into foxes.
   b. The strong dogs became working animals.
   c. The strong dogs did not like to work hard.

6. The main idea of the whole story is that
   a. dogs and people have been friends for a long time.
   b. foxes are better than dogs for pulling heavy loads.
   c. all animals cannot be pets.

7. The opposite of *weak* (paragraph four, sentence one) is _____.

A Horse No Bigger Than a Cat

1   Have you ever seen a horse with toes? Millions of years ago, horses had many toes. They had four toes on each front foot. They had three toes on each back foot. The horses were no bigger than cats.

2   These small horses lived in the forest. Their many toes helped the horses run over the soft, wet ground.

3   It was very hot in the forest. But the weather changed. It became cold. Many trees could not live in cold weather. The trees died and fell. Open fields took the place of forests. The sun made the ground dry and hard.

4   Horses began to change, too. They began to get bigger. This took a long time. On the dry, hard land, horses needed only their middle toes for running. Their middle toes became hard. After a long while, horses had only one hard toe on each foot. We call this hard toe a hoof.

30

1. Long ago, the horse had four toes on each of its
   a. front feet. c. back feet.
   b. left feet. d. right feet.

2. The word in the story that means *many trees together* is

   _____.

3. The story says, "But the weather changed. *It* became cold."

   The word *it* means _____.

4. Which of the following does this story lead you to believe?
   a. Animals have always been the same as they are today.
   b. When the earth changed, animals began to change, too.
   c. Weather stays the same all year long around the world.

5. What did the horses need on dry, hard land? (Which sentence is exactly like the one in your book?)
   a. On the dry, hard land, horses needed only their middle toes for running.
   b. On the dry, hard land, the horses needed a lot of room for running.
   c. On the dry, hard land, horses needed to get smaller.

6. The main idea of the whole story is that
   a. the weather never changes.
   b. cats were once much bigger than horses.
   c. horses changed very much over the years.

7. The opposite of *dry* (in sentence seven) is _____.

The Smallest Bird

1   The little bird took nectar from a flower. This sweet liquid was food for the bird. It used its long bill to get at the nectar deep in the flower. The little bird was a hummingbird. Hummingbirds are the smallest birds in the world.

2   The hummingbird made a nest. The nest looked like a very small cup. Soon there were two white eggs in the nest. The eggs were no bigger than peas. Little birds came out of the eggs. They were very hungry. The parent birds brought them nectar. They put their long bills down the necks of the babies to feed them nectar.

3   The baby birds stayed in the nest almost three weeks. They left the nest when they were big enough and strong enough to fly. Soon they could build their own nests. They could get their own nectar. They could feed their own very small babies.

1. The hummingbird got nectar from a
   a. nest.   c. bird.
   b. flower.   d. cup.

2. The word in the story that means *the smallest bird in the world*

   is _____ .

3. The story says, "Little birds came out of the eggs. *They* were very

   hungry." The word *they* means _____ .

4. Which of the following does this story lead you to believe?
   a. Hummingbirds have to eat only green peas to stay alive.
   b. Hummingbirds need the nectar from flowers to stay alive.
   c. Hummingbirds don't know how to make nests.

5. How big were the hummingbird's eggs? (Which sentence is
   exactly like the one in your book?)
   a. The eggs were no bigger than peas.
   b. The eggs were no bigger than cups.
   c. The eggs were no bigger than marbles.

6. The main idea of the whole story is that
   a. hummingbirds are big birds.
   b. birds' nests are made out of tiny green peas.
   c. the mother bird takes care of the baby birds.

7. The opposite of *left* (paragraph three, sentence one) is

   _____ .

Room to Grow

1   Lightning hit a giant tree in the forest. The tree died. It fell to the ground. Soon the tree began to rot.

2   Seeds from other trees fell to the ground. These seeds could not grow. There were too many plants on the forest floor. But one seed fell on the dead tree. It was high off the ground. This seed had room to grow.

3   A new plant grew from the seed that fell on the dead tree. The new plant put out new roots. The roots grew into the rotting tree. The roots went through the tree to the ground.

4   The dead tree rotted more and more. But the new plant grew. The rotting tree was its food. The new plant reached for the sun. It grew tall and strong. Soon there was another tree in the forest.

1. When a tree dies and falls to the ground it begins to
   - a. rot.
   - b. grow.
   - c. bleed.
   - d. bite.

2. The word in the story that means *the ground in the forest on which many plants grow* is _____.

3. The story says, "The tree died. *It* fell to the ground." The word *it* means _____.

4. Which of the following does this story lead you to believe?
   - a. Seeds do not need room to grow.
   - b. Some seeds plant themselves.
   - c. Seeds make trees die.

5. Where did one seed fall? (Which sentence is exactly like the one in your book?)
   - a. But one seed fell on the dead tree.
   - b. But one seed fell on a new plant.
   - c. But one seed was hit by lightning.

6. The main idea of the whole story is that
   - a. a new plant can grow out of a dead plant.
   - b. lightning cannot hit a tree.
   - c. seeds do not need room to grow well.

7. The opposite of *low* (paragraph two, sentence five) is _____.

The Frog That Changes Color

1   Birds live in trees. Squirrels live in trees. But did you know that some frogs live in trees, too?

2   The tree frog is hard to find. This frog can change color. On green leaves, it stays green. On a brown branch, it turns brown. Some tree frogs can change from green to gold or blue.

3   Tree frogs have long legs and wide feet. They have sticky pads at the ends of their toes. These sticky toe pads keep the tree frogs from falling.

4   Tree frogs have different colors and markings on their skins. Their eyes are different, too. Some have green eyes, some gray. Some frogs' eyes are gold, and some are bright red.

5   The sounds they make in spring and summer are different, too. One frog makes a sound like a dog barking. Another frog makes a loud noise like a snore. There is even a frog that whistles!

1. Tree frogs have sticky pads on the ends of their
    a. noses.   c. arms.
    b. tails.   d. toes.

2. The word in the story that means *different signs on an animal's*
    skin is _____.

3. The story says, "This frog can change color. On green leaves, *it*
    stays green." The word *it* means _____.

4. Which of the following does this story lead you to believe?
    a. There are many different kinds of frogs.
    b. All frogs have red eyes and make the same sound.
    c. Frogs all look the same.

5. Why is the tree frog hard to find? (Which sentence is exactly
    like the one in your book?)
    a. This frog can stand on its toes.
    b. This frog can make a dog bark.
    c. This frog can change color.

6. The main idea of the whole story is that
    a. squirrels do not want frogs in their trees.
    b. the tree frog is a special kind of frog.
    c. dogs bark like frogs.

7. The opposite of *short* (paragraph three, sentence one) is

    _____.

Let's Trade

1   Let's trade! Will you take a piece of cake for an apple? A good book for a game? A toy boat for a car?

2   Long ago, people had to get what they wanted by trading. Some people farmed the land. Other people made tools. Tools were traded for food.

3   All kinds of trading took place. If people had too much meat, they could trade it for corn. They could trade animal skins for tools. Sometimes a person would trade a day's work for a place to sleep.

4   Many useful things were traded. But people wanted pretty things, too. A farmer might trade milk for a piece of beautiful cloth.

5   Even today we trade with one another. When you buy candy, do you pay for it with bear fat? Of course not! You use money. But you are still trading. You are still giving one thing for another.

1. A day's work was traded for
    a. a place to sleep.   c. games.
    b. an apple.   d. toy boats.

2. The word in the story that means *giving one thing for another*

    is _____.

3. The story says, "If people had too much meat, they could trade

    it for corn." The word *it* means _____.

4. Which of the following does this story lead you to believe?
    a. Long ago, people might trade a pig for a piece of silk.
    b. People long ago used to trade bear fat for animals.
    c. People long ago didn't know very much about trading.

5. How do you trade today? (Which sentence is exactly like the one
    in your book?)
    a. You use money.
    b. You use chickens.
    c. You trade when you hear a bell ring.

6. The main idea of the whole story is that
    a. people trade only for food and a place to sleep.
    b. people never traded any useful things long ago.
    c. people trade things for what they need and want.

7. The opposite of *yesterday* (paragraph five, sentence one) is

    _____.

A Thread 100 Miles Long

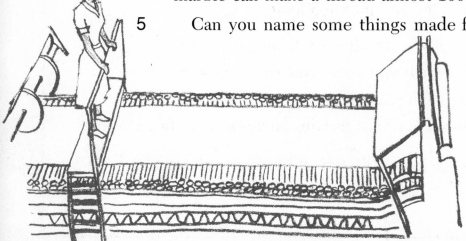

1   Would you wear leaves or grass? Would you wear an animal skin? No? Long ago, people had to wear what they could find. They had no cloth.

2   Would you wear coal or milk or grain? No, again? Are you sure?

3   Ways have been found to use these things for clothes. Milk or coal or grain may be put with other things and cooked. The heat turns these things into a liquid. The liquid runs out through little holes. Now, it becomes long threads. The threads are fine and strong. Cloth is made from the threads.

4   Today, cloth can even be made from glass. First the glass is shaped into marbles. These are made very hot in a machine. The machine has many little holes. The marbles are pushed through the holes. Glass from the marbles comes out in long threads. One glass marble can make a thread almost 100 miles long!

5   Can you name some things made from glass thread?

1. Cloth can be made from
   a. bananas.   c. holes.
   b. glass.   d. clay.

2. The word in the story that means *something that is not solid* is _____.

3. The story says "Long ago, people had to wear what *they* could find." The word *they* means _____.

4. Which of the following does this story lead you to believe?
   a. Glass thread can be made to make many things.
   b. Animals have to wear clothes made of grass.
   c. No one can make threads that are long.

5. What are the threads like? (Which sentence is exactly like the one in your book?)
   a. The threads are fine and strong.
   b. The threads are thin and long.
   c. The threads are much too long.

6. The main idea of the whole story is that
   a. people can only use milk and grain for food.
   b. different things have been used to make clothes.
   c. machines become 100 miles long when making cloth.

7. The opposite of *big* (paragraph three, sentence four) is _____.

When Jaws Can't Bite

1   There is a woman who sits on the floor of the ocean. She's waiting for sharks! Eugenie Clark is a famous scientist. She studied sharks for twenty years.

2   She tells us that sharks eat every kind of fish. But there is one they won't eat. It is a small fish that lives in the Red Sea, near Egypt. It is called the Red Sea sole.

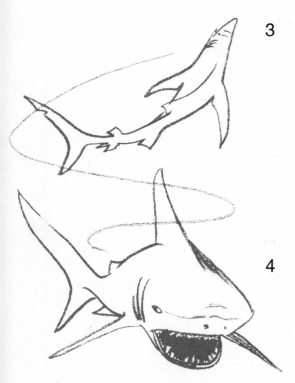

3   The shark hunts many fish to eat. It may swim closer and closer to a Red Sea sole. Then, it opens its mouth to eat the little fish. Suddenly, the sole sends out a poison. Now, the shark can't even close its mouth! It shakes its head back and forth. It swims away. The little fish is safe.

4   The shark scientist may use this fish poison to keep sharks away from people. Maybe some day we will spray sharks away just as we do bugs!

1. Sharks like to eat
   - a. poison.
   - b. fish.
   - c. bugs.
   - d. sole.

2. The word in the story that means *stuff that can kill* is

   _____ .

3. The story says, "Now, the shark can't even close its mouth."

   The word *its* means _____ .

4. Which of the following does this story lead you to believe?
   - a. Diving into the ocean keeps sharks away.
   - b. Sharks hate little fish.
   - c. Most fish cannot keep sharks from biting.

5. Why does the shark stay away from the Red Sea sole? (Which sentence is exactly like the one in your book?)
   - a. The Red Sea sole bites back.
   - b. Red sharks don't live near Egypt.
   - c. Suddenly the sole sends out a poison.

6. The main idea of the whole story is that
   - a. people should stay out of the ocean.
   - b. scientists like to stay under water.
   - c. scientists can teach us more about sharks.

7. The opposite of *closes* (in paragraph three, sentence three) is

   _____ .

Walking, Talking Ads

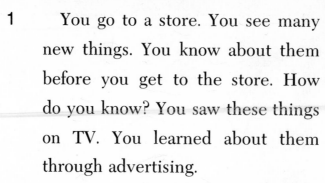

1   You go to a store. You see many new things. You know about them before you get to the store. How do you know? You saw these things on TV. You learned about them through advertising.

2   People have been advertising for thousands of years. Long ago, men called "criers" walked up and down the streets. They shouted about things that were being sold.

3   Later, people met at one place. This place was a market. Some people came to sell. Other people came to buy. But only those people who were at the market knew what was being sold.

4   When people learned about printing, things changed. Soon there were newspapers. Many people read the newspapers. They saw many ads in the papers. Later, more people saw and listened to the ads on TV. Are the people who sell to us "criers"?

1. When you go to a store you see
   a. singers.
   c. many new things.
   b. people crying.
   d. dancers.

2. The word in the story that means *papers printed every day that tell the news* is ___newspaper___ .

3. The story says, "Many people read the newspapers. *They* saw many ads in the papers." The word *they* means _____ .

4. Which of the following does this story lead you to believe?
   a. We go to the store to read the newspaper.
   b. We go to the store to buy things we hear about.
   c. We go to the store to look at the ads on television.

5. How long have people been advertising? (Which sentence is exactly like the one in your book?)
   a. People have been advertising since yesterday.
   b. People have not been advertising very much at all.
   c. People have been advertising for thousands of years.

6. The main idea of the whole story is that
   a. people advertise to sell things.
   b. people cried when they had to advertise.
   c. people went to the market.

7. The opposite of *sell* (paragraph three, sentence four) is

   _____ .

Can You Vote?

1   You know that men and women vote. They vote for the people who run our country. But did you know that you vote, too? Did you know that your vote is very important?

2   You go to the store. Your parent picks up a box of cereal. You say, "No! Not that one!" You pick another cereal. You have just voted for one cereal. You have just voted against another cereal. If enough people vote against a cereal, it does not sell. Soon the company must stop making this cereal. Your vote makes this happen.

3   You see a new toy. You buy it. You don't like it. You tell your friends not to buy it. Soon the toy company cannot sell this toy. It makes a different toy that you will want to own.

4   You are very important. You are the one with the vote.

1. You vote against something by saying
   a. hello.   c. maybe.
   b. good-by.   d. no.

2. The word in the story that means *to choose one thing and not the other* is _____ .

3. The story says, "You see a new toy. You buy *it*." The word *it* means _____ .

4. Which of the following does this story lead you to believe?
   a. A toy company won't let you buy a toy you like very much.
   b. A toy company takes all your toys away to fix them.
   c. A toy company keeps trying to make toys you will like.

5. What happens when your parent goes to the store? (Which sentence is exactly like the one in your book?)
   a. Your parent looks at toys on TV.
   b. Your parent runs the country.
   c. Your parent picks up a box of cereal.

6. The main idea of the whole story is that
   a. we can buy all our cereals in a store.
   b. we can vote for or against something.
   c. your vote is not important.

7. The opposite of *against* (paragraph two, sentence five) is _____ .

The Hat That Talked

1   Every winter the Indians caught beavers. They sold the beaver furs to people from France. In the 1600s and 1700s, people in France wanted beaver furs for coats and hats. Other countries wanted these furs, too. Wearing a beaver fur hat became a sign. It said, "Look at this person! This person is rich!"

2   In the 1800s, men and women in this country began to wear beaver hats. They, too, wanted to wear the sign that said, "Look at us! We are rich!"

3   To get more beaver furs, traders had to move West. Traders began to explore this new country. They came back with wonderful stories about the new land. Soon many people wanted to go West to live.

4   It became very hard to find beavers. Many of them had been killed in the hunt for fancy hats. But there were many new towns in the West. People looking for beaver for hats helped the West grow.

1. Wearing a beaver hat was a sign that a person was
    a. a hunter.
    c. a trader.
    b. rich.
    d. an Indian.

2. The word in the story that means *a person who trades things* is

    _____ .

3. The story says, "Every winter the Indians caught beavers. *They* sold these beaver furs to people from France." The word *they*

    means _____ .

4. Which of the following does this story lead you to believe?
    a. Beavers began to wear fancy hats.
    b. The traders would not go West.
    c. The fur traders helped our country grow.

5. What did the traders do when beavers were hard to find? (Which sentence is exactly like the one in your book?)
    a. To get more beaver furs, traders had to move West.
    b. Traders had to find rich people wearing signs.
    c. The traders had to wear beaver hats out West.

6. The main idea of the whole story is that
    a. traders carried signs for rich people.
    b. the search for beavers helped the West to grow.
    c. many wonderful stories were told about the West.

7. The opposite of *East* (paragraph three, sentence two) is

    _____ .

The Tree That Was Always Different

A man and his four children lived in a hot country. Here the trees were always green. One day, the man and his children moved to a different land. This land had four seasons. Soon after they came, the four children heard about a beautiful tree. It was called the redbud. Each child wanted very much to see this tree.

One day in early spring, the man went to the woods. The oldest son went, too. "Father," he said, "where is the redbud?"

"There," said the father. The oldest son was surprised. The tree had no leaves! He wondered why it was called a redbud. But he did not ask.

In late spring, the father showed the oldest daughter the redbud. It was bright with many flowers.

"How beautiful it is!" the daughter cried.

In early summer, the third child went with his father to the woods. "Look!" said the father. "There is the redbud!"

"It is just a tree with green leaves," the third child thought. "I wonder why it is called a redbud." But he did not ask.

51

At last, in the fall, the youngest daughter went to the woods. "Father," she said, "show me the redbud."

"There," said the father.

"It is just a tree with leaves and little bean pods," the youngest child thought. She wondered why it was called a redbud. "If I ask, my father will think I know nothing." So she kept quiet. But as soon as she was home, she ran to the others. "I have seen the redbud," she said. "It is not beautiful. It just has leaves and bean pods."

"That is not the redbud," the oldest son said. "The redbud has no leaves."

"What?" cried the second son. "Of course it has leaves. But it does not have bean pods."

"Bean pods? What tree have you seen?" asked the oldest daughter. "The redbud is covered with beautiful flowers."

Just then the father came up to them. He was laughing. "You have all seen the same tree. But you have seen it at different times. In early spring, the redbud has no leaves. Then it has beautiful flowers. After the flowers fall, the leaves come out. Now it has bean pods."

The children looked at each other. They laughed, too. "We were all right. And we were all wrong," the oldest brother said. "We have learned one thing! There is more than one way to look at something!"

409 words

The Rain Dance

1   The land was dry. The Indians looked at the sky. There were no clouds. "We must have rain," the Indians said. So they danced a rain dance. They thought this would bring rain. They danced with snakes. Then they let the snakes go. "Go back into the ground," they said to the snakes. "Tell the gods to make the rain come."

2   Can people make rain fall? Sometimes. But a rain dance will not bring rain. Today, to make rain, people go up in airplanes. They take dry ice with them. They spread the dry ice on the clouds. This is called seeding the clouds. Drops of water in the clouds become ice. The ice melts and makes big rain drops.

3   Seeding clouds does not always make the rain fall. Rain falls only if the clouds are big and full of water.

1. The Indians thought they could get rain by
   a. seeding the clouds.   c. looking at the sky.
   b. melting ice.   d. dancing with snakes.

2. The word in the story that means *spreading dry ice on clouds to make rain* is _____ .

3. The story says, "Today, to make rain, people go up in airplanes. *They* take dry ice with them." The word *they* means _____ .

4. Which of the following does this story lead you to believe?
   a. People are learning more about how to make rain.
   b. Dry ice helps snakes talk to the gods.
   c. Seeding clouds always makes the rain fall.

5. When will the rain fall? (Which sentence is exactly like the one in your book?)
   a. Rain falls only when Indians dance with a snake.
   b. Rain falls only if the clouds are big and full of water.
   c. Rain falls only if there are no clouds in the sky.

6. The main idea of the whole story is that
   a. seeds make plants grow in the clouds.
   b. we must have rain.
   c. snakes are found in airplanes.

7. The opposite of *never* (paragraph three) is _____ .

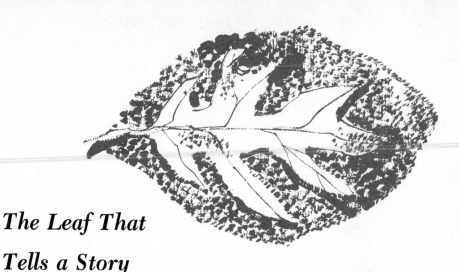

The Leaf That Tells a Story

1   A hundred million years ago, a leaf fell to the ground. It landed in soft mud. More mud covered the leaf. After a long time the mud dried. Rocks and water pressed down on it.

2   Years passed. The dirt around the leaf was pressed to stone. The leaf became dust. But it had left a mark on the stone. The mark was shaped like the leaf. It was a fossil.

3   There are many kinds of fossils. Sometimes a whole animal became a fossil. Some fossils are shaped like fish. Some are shaped like birds.

4   Today, scientists look at the fossils. From the fossils, scientists can learn what kind of trees grew long ago. They can tell what kind of animals once lived on earth.

5   Fossils can be found in many places. Look at the rocks you pick up. You may find a fossil. It may be one hundred million years old!

FIND THE ANSWERS

1. By looking at fossils, scientists can learn about
   a. long ago.   c. stones.
   b. tomorrow.   d. water.

2. The word in the story that means *fell to the ground* is

   _____.

3. The story says, "You may find a fossil. *It* may be one hundred

   million years old!" The word *it* means _____.

4. Which of the following does the story lead you to believe?
   a. Fossils are shaped like people, birds, and animals.
   b. Fossils tell us what the earth was like long ago.
   c. Fossils are always hard to find.

5. What can fossils tell us? (Which sentence is exactly like the
   one in your book?)
   a. They can tell us which animals people ate.
   b. They can tell us how many animals lived on the earth.
   c. They can tell what kind of animals once lived on earth.

6. The main idea of the whole story is that
   a. fossils tell a story about the earth.
   b. you can pick up rocks in many places.
   c. scientists cannot learn anything from fossils.

7. The opposite of *died* (paragraph four, sentence three) is

   _____.

The Fish on the Mountain

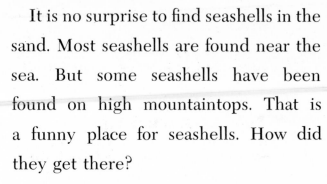

1   It is no surprise to find seashells in the sand. Most seashells are found near the sea. But some seashells have been found on high mountaintops. That is a funny place for seashells. How did they get there?

2   The earth did not always look the way it does today. Once the sea covered more of the land. Then mountains pushed up. They pushed up through the water. Land from the bottom of the sea became mountaintops. Seashells and fish bones were pushed up, too. They were far away from sea water. They were left high and dry.

3   The seashells and fish bones were covered with soft mud and sand. The mud became hard. It turned to stone. The shapes of the shell and bones were pressed into the stone. These stones are called fossils.

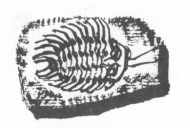

4   Fossils have been found all over our country. Have you ever found one?

1. Some seashells have been found
   - a. in trees.
   - b. on mountaintops.
   - c. on roads.
   - d. in the air.

2. The word in the story that means *shapes of bones pressed into stone* is _____.

3. The story says, "The earth did not always look the way *it* does today." The word *it* means _____.

4. Which of the following does this story lead you to believe?
   - a. Fish began to live in trees.
   - b. Fossils can be found far away from the sea.
   - c. Seashells turned into fish bones.

5. What happened to seashells and fish bones? (Which sentence is exactly like the one in your book?)
   - a. They were left under the water.
   - b. Seashells and fish bones were left far from the water.
   - c. Seashells and fish bones were pushed up, too.

6. The main idea of the whole story is that
   - a. seashells are funny.
   - b. mud turns into stone.
   - c. the earth has changed.

7. The opposite of *lost* (in paragraph four) is _____.

A River of Ice

1   Snow fell on the mountain. It snowed and snowed. The snow did not melt. It became deep and heavy. The snow on the bottom pressed together. It became ice.

2   The ice was very wide and thick. It began to move down the mountain. It was like a river of ice. It was a glacier.

3   Sometimes the glacier moved only a few inches each day. As it moved, it took rocks and dirt with it. It changed the land. In some places, it left hills. In some places, when the glacier melted, it made rivers and lakes.

4   A million years ago, there were many big glaciers. Glaciers covered many parts of the world. The glaciers changed the land.

5   Glaciers are still at work today. A glacier in the north of Canada is cutting a new path down the side of a mountain. This glacier will change the land, too.

1. The snow that fell on the mountain
   a. became snowmen.   c. melted.
   b. became ice.   d. turned to rain.

2. The word in the story that means *a river of ice* is _____ .

3. The story says, "The snow did not melt. *It* became deep and heavy." The word *it* means _____ .

4. Which of the following does this story lead you to believe?
   a. There are not as many glaciers as there used to be.
   b. Glaciers do not change the land as they move over it.
   c. Glaciers are found only in warm places.

5. How fast did the glacier move? (Which sentence is exactly like the one in your book?)
   a. Sometimes the glacier moved only once a year.
   b. Sometimes the glacier moved over ten miles each day.
   c. Sometimes the glacier moved only a few inches each day.

6. The main idea of the whole story is that
   a. snow is heavy.
   b. the high land never changes.
   c. glaciers changed the land.

7. The opposite of *south* (paragraph five, sentence two) is _____ .

The River That Dug a Canyon

1 The Colorado River has been working for millions of years. It has been digging the Grand Canyon.

2 At first, the water was even with the land on each side. The water raced along. It carried dirt and rocks with it. Each year the water cut away a little more of the land. The river bed became deep. Today the river is at the bottom of the Grand Canyon.

3 Many people visit the Grand Canyon. Some people ride mules down the sides of the canyon. They pass layers of rock cut by the river. The layers are different colors. The colors tell many things. They tell how the land was built up before the river began to cut through it.

4 The Colorado River is still racing along at the bottom of the canyon. It is still digging away at the Grand Canyon.

FIND THE ANSWERS

1. The layers of rock in the Grand Canyon are
   a. mule paths.
   b. the river bed.
   c. different colors.
   d. at the bottom.

2. The word in the story that means *a deep valley* is _____.

3. The story says, "The water raced along. *It* carried dirt and rocks with it." The word *it* means _____.

4. Which of the following does this story lead you to believe?
   a. Years from now the Grand Canyon may be much deeper.
   b. Both people and mules live in the Grand Canyon.
   c. The Grand Canyon is not very deep any more.

5. What is the Colorado River still doing? (Which sentence is exactly like the one in your book?)
   a. It is still flowing along through the Grand Canyon.
   b. It is still turning different colors.
   c. It is still digging away at the Grand Canyon.

6. The main idea of the whole story is that
   a. rocks have colors.
   b. a river dug the Grand Canyon.
   c. mules ride in the Colorado River.

7. The opposite of *after* (paragraph three, sentence six) is

   _____.

Volcano in a Field

1   Most mountains are very old. They were here before there were people. But some mountains are still being made. They are volcanoes.

2   Mexico has a new mountain. It began in 1943 near the town of Parícutin (pə rē´kə tēn). The mountain grew in a field. The ground began to shake. Part of the ground opened. Smoke and hot rocks came out of the opening. The hot rocks began to build up into a big hill. The hill was shaped like a cone.

3   Out of the cone came hot melted rock. This melted rock was lava. It moved like a river. It ran down the sides of the cone. It covered more and more of the land. Soon it covered the town of Parícutin. In the open air, the lava became cold and hard.

4   At last, in 1952, lava stopped coming from the volcano. Mexico had a new, small mountain.

1. The new mountain was made
   - a. by a river.
   - c. in Mexico.
   - b. by people.
   - d. in America.

2. The word in the story that means *hot, melted rock* is

   _____ .

3. The story says, "Most mountains are very old. *They* were here before there were people." The word *they* means

   _____ .

4. Which of the following does this story lead you to believe?
   - a. Dogs and children liked to play in the hot lava.
   - b. Many people in Parícutin had to leave their homes.
   - c. The new mountain made the people in town very happy.

5. What happened to the lava in the open air? (Which sentence is exactly like the one in your book?)
   - a. In the open air, the lava turned into fish eggs.
   - b. In the open air, the lava became cold and hard.
   - c. In the open air, the lava turned to rain.

6. The main idea of the whole story is that
   - a. new mountains are still being made.
   - b. people in Mexico like lava.
   - c. people are older than mountains.

7. The opposite of *closed* (paragraph two, sentence five) is

   _____ .

How Cities Began

1   Do you live in a city? Do you know how cities began? Long ago, the world had only a few thousand people. These people moved from place to place. They moved over the land, hunting animals for food.

2   No one knows how or when these people learned about growing food. But when they did, their lives changed. They did not have to look for food any more. They could stay in one place and grow it.

3   People began to live near one another. And so the first villages grew. Many people came to work in the villages. These villages grew very big.

4   When machines came along, life in the villages changed again. Factories were built. More and more people lived near the factories. The cities grew very big.

5   Today, some people are moving back to small towns. Can you tell why?

FIND THE ANSWERS

1. People moved from place to place hunting
   - a. animals.
   - c. machines.
   - b. villages.
   - d. factories.

2. The word in the story that means *found out about something* is _____ .

3. The story says, "No one knows how or when these people learned about growing food. But when *they* did, their lives changed." The word *they* means _____ .

4. Which of the following does this story lead you to believe?
   - a. All people like to live only in very big cities.
   - b. It is good to live near a factory.
   - c. Some people do not like to live in big cities.

5. What happened when factories were built? (Which sentence is exactly like the one in your book?)
   - a. People began to live in the factories.
   - b. More and more people lived near the factories.
   - c. There are many machines in big city factories.

6. The main idea of the whole story is that
   - a. factories were built after the cities grew big.
   - b. people like to eat when they visit big cities.
   - c. cities began when people lived and worked near each other.

7. The opposite of *to* (in sentence four) is _____ .

A Bag of Bugs

1   When you are sick, you go to a doctor. Where do you go when your tooth hurts? What do you think people did long ago when they were sick?

2   Make believe you are a child of long ago. You are sick. What do you do?

3   Are you coughing? Put a bag of live bugs around your neck. Does your neck hurt? Put pepper on a piece of fat. Now tie the fat around your neck. Do you have warts? Dig a hole in the ground. Put your mother's dishcloth in it. The warts will go away.

4   Does a tooth need pulling? Tie a string around it. Tie one end of the string to a branch of a small tree. Let the branch go. There goes your tooth!

5   These were some things people did long ago when they were sick. Aren't you glad you don't have to wear a bag of bugs?

68

1. When you are sick, you go to
   a. a store.   c. a baker.
   b. a park.   d. a doctor.

2. The word in the story that means *a cloth used for washing dishes*
   is _____ .

3. The story says, "What do you think people did long ago when *they*
   were sick?" The word *they* means _____ .

4. Which of the following does this story lead you to believe?
   a. A bag of bugs can make you well.
   b. Sick people want to get well.
   c. It's fun to be sick.

5. What could you do if you had a cough? (Which sentence is exactly
   like the one in your book?)
   a. Swing on the branch of a small tree.
   b. Eat fat with pepper on it.
   c. Put a bag of live bugs around your neck.

6. The main idea of the whole story is that
   a. children of long ago liked pepper.
   b. sick people tried many things to get well.
   c. doctors want you to wear bugs around your neck.

7. The opposite of *sad* (paragraph five, sentence two) is _____ .

Are You a Little Doll?

1   Long ago, people in Rome talked to one another in Latin. Pupils in school learned to read and write Latin. Books were in Latin.

2   Some Romans went to other parts of the world. They took their language with them. Soon Latin was used in many countries. It became a world language.

3   People in other countries did not talk Latin the same way. In each land, they changed the language a little. As time went by, they made more changes. At last they did not speak in Latin any more. New languages had come from the old one.

4   People do not talk to one another in Latin today. But they still use many Latin words. You do, too. *Street, wall, city,* and *salt* are some of the Latin words we use. You are a pupil in school. *Pupil* is a Latin word. It means "little doll."

1. Latin was used by people in
   a. Rome.
   c. the United States.
   b. Greece.
   d. Texas.

2. The word in the story that means *what people speak and write*

   is _____.

3. The story says, "People do not talk to each other in Latin today. But *they* still use many Latin words." The word *they* means

   _____.

4. Which of the following does this story lead you to believe?
   a. It is not good to change a language.
   b. Pupils in schools today play with dolls.
   c. Not many people can read Latin today.

5. What happened to Latin when it was taken to other countries? (Which sentence is exactly like the one in your book?)
   a. In each land, people talked about each other.
   b. In each land, they changed the language a little.
   c. In each land, the children had to speak some Latin.

6. The main idea of the whole story is that
   a. Romans did not like to stay home.
   b. people in old Rome talked a lot to each other.
   c. Latin changed as it moved from land to land.

7. The opposite of *first* (in paragraph three, sentence four) is

   _____.

Please Pass the Pepper

1   Long ago, some people in Europe went to fight a war. The war was in Asia. These people lost the war. But they came back with many new things.

cinnamon

2   They brought back glass. They brought silk. And they brought back spices. Pepper and cinnamon were some of the spices.

3   People in Asia had used spices for a long time. But before the war in Asia, people in Europe knew nothing about spices. Once they tasted spices on their food, they wanted more. But spices were hard to get. Having lost the war, people could not go to Asia by land. They had to find other ways to get there. They looked for a way to go by sea.

pepper

4   They did not find their way to Asia. But they found something else. They found America. Many people left their own countries. They came to America to live.

5   Because of spices, the lives of some people changed.

1. The war was in
    a. South America.   c. Asia.
    b. North America.   d. the United States.

2. The word in the story that means *pepper and cinnamon* is

    _____.

3. The story says, "Many people left their own countries. *They* came

    to America to live." The word *they* means _____.

4. Which of the following does this story lead you to believe?
    a. Looking for one thing may lead to finding something else.
    b. People cannot live in their own countries.
    c. People in Europe had known about spices for many years.

5. What happened when the people of Europe tasted spices? (Which
    sentence is exactly like the one in your book?)
    a. Once they tasted spices on their food, they wanted more.
    b. Once they tasted spices, they ate all their food.
    c. Once they tasted spices, they would not eat.

6. The main idea of the whole story is that
    a. the people of Europe wanted spices.
    b. glass and silk are better than spices.
    c. pepper is hard to get.

7. The opposite of *sea* (paragraph three, sentence five) is

    _____.

Send a Message

1   An Indian put her ear to the ground. She heard many horses. They were coming her way. She ran to tell her people. Then she ran to tell the people of the next village. She was a runner. Using runners was one way Indians sent messages.

2   People in a land across the sea sent messages, too. One man beat his drum. In the next village the people heard the drum. They beat their drums. The message went from village to village by drums.

3   Much later, some armies kept many pigeons. These pigeons always flew back to their own nesting place. Suppose a soldier was sent far from his own army. He might take a pigeon along. He could tie a message to the bird's leg. He would let the bird go. It would fly home with the soldier's message.

4   These were slow ways to send messages. Can you think of fast ways?

1. When the Indian listened for horses, she put her ear to the
   a. tree.   c. table.
   b. water.   d. ground.

2. The word in the story that means *a person who carries a message*

   is _____ .

3. The story says, "An Indian put her ear to the ground. *She*

   heard many horses." The word *she* means _____ .

4. Which of the following does this story lead you to believe?
   a. People have always used pigeons to send messages.
   b. Pigeons like soldiers who send messages.
   c. There are better ways to send messages today.

5. How could a soldier use a pigeon to send a message? (Which
   sentence is exactly like the one in your book?)
   a. He could tie a pigeon to his leg.
   b. He could tie a message to the bird's leg.
   c. He could fly the message home with a pigeon.

6. The main idea of the whole story is that
   a. Indians run a lot to carry messages.
   b. people like to beat drums to make music.
   c. messages have been sent in many ways.

7. The opposite of *fast* (paragraph four, sentence one) is

   _____ .

When Schools Were Different

1   Does your teacher live with you? In pioneer days, a teacher took turns living with each child's family.

2   Sometimes in schools, children did not listen to the teacher. Then they had to wear tall paper hats called dunce caps. Sometimes children had to stand in corners facing the wall. Other times they had to sit in odd places.

3   The teacher had a chair and table. The children sat on log benches. There were no desks. Many times the boys sat on one bench and the girls on another. Children had slates to write on. But sometimes they went to the "writing table." This was a board in one corner of the room. Here, children could write on paper with pen and ink.

4   Pioneer children made their own pens and ink. Pens were made from turkey feathers. The hard part of the feather was made into a point. Ink was made from berries.

5   How different is your school today?

FIND THE ANSWERS

1. Children made pens from
   a. berries.   c. turkey feathers.
   b. logs.   d. sticks.

2. The word in the story that means *hats* is _____.

3. The story says, "Children had slates to write on. But sometimes *they* went to the 'writing table.'" The word *they* means

   _____.

4. Which of the following does this story lead you to believe?
   a. Our schools are better than the pioneer schools.
   b. It is good to write on slates in schools.
   c. Boards are kept in corners for children to sit on.

5. What did the children sit on? (Which sentence is exactly like the one in your book?)
   a. The children sat on log benches.
   b. The children sat on the writing tables.
   c. The children sat on the floor.

6. The main idea of the whole story is that
   a. pioneer children made their own log benches.
   b. children need turkey feathers to make their own pens.
   c. pioneer schools were very different from our schools.

7. The opposite of *stand* (paragraph two, sentence four) is _____.

Changing Lines

1   What is it? Sometimes it is long. Sometimes it is round. There may be only one. There may be more of them than you can count. You can make a sign for it. The sign will look like this _____. Now you can guess. It is a line.

2   Sometimes a line is straight _____ \ /. Some lines are side by side. They never meet ═══════. Train tracks are like these lines.

3   Some lines do meet. The lines cross each other ─╫────╫─ Streets are like lines that cross each other.

4   When lines change, new shapes are made. Sometimes a line is curved. Curved lines may cross each other ⟨. Curved lines may be side by side ⌒. Curved lines may be closed. A circle is one kind of closed curve.

5   Look about you. Can you find straight lines and curved lines? Can you find lines that cross and lines that do not cross?

1. A circle is one kind of a

    a. street.   c. closed curve.
    b. straight line.   d. sign.

2. The word in the story that means *going from one side over to another* is _____.

3. The story says, "Some lines are side by side. *They* never meet." The word *they* means _____.

4. Which of the following does this story lead you to believe?
    a. All lines are straight and long.
    b. All lines look like train tracks.
    c. Lines are used by man in many ways.

5. What happens when lines change? (Which sentence is exactly like the one in your book?)
    a. When lines change, new shapes are made.
    b. When lines change, streets have to cross each other.
    c. When lines change, they get crossed.

6. The main idea of the whole story is that
    a. there are many kinds of lines.
    b. lines must never meet.
    c. streets cannot cross each other.

7. The opposite of *curved* (paragraph two, sentence one) is

    _____.

A Stone for a Sheep

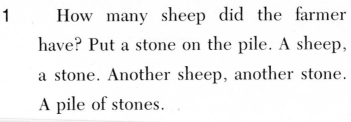

1 How many sheep did the farmer have? Put a stone on the pile. A sheep, a stone. Another sheep, another stone. A pile of stones.

2 How many animals did the hunter kill? Make a cut in a stick. Make a big cut for a lion. Make a small cut for a bird.

3 How many days ago was the seed planted? Tie a knot in a rope each day. One day, one knot. Many days, many knots.

4 Once there were no words for numerals. People could not tell how many. They could match a sheep to a stone. They could match a cut in a stick to each animal. But they could not count.

5 After a while people had a word for one, for two, for three, for many. They counted, "One, two, three, many." More than three were many. Today, we can count any number of things and tell exactly how many.

1. A farmer counted sheep with
   a. seeds.
   b. cuts in sticks.
   c. birds.
   d. stones.

2. The word in the story that means *1, 2, 3, 4,* and *5* is _____ .

3. The story says, "People could not tell how many. *They* could match a sheep to a stone." The word *they* means _____ .

4. Which of the following does this story lead you to believe?
   a. Piling stones is the best way to count.
   b. People can count better with numerals.
   c. Knots in ropes help seeds grow.

5. What words did people long ago use in counting? (Which sentence is exactly like the one in your book?)
   a. They counted how many sheep made knots.
   b. They counted many more than three.
   c. They counted, "One, two, three, many."

6. The main idea of the whole story is that
   a. hunters killed animals.
   b. people learned to count.
   c. farmers had lots of stones.

7. The opposite of *many* (paragraph three, sentence three) is

   _____ .

The Year the Barn Burned Down

1   Have you ever heard people say, "I remember that. That was the year the cow fell through the ice"? Or "That was the year the barn burned down"?

2   Indians counted years this way. They would draw pictures on animal skins. The pictures named the years that some big thing took place. They might tell of "the fire that killed the animals" summer. Or "the rivers that covered the land" spring.

3   Long ago, years were remembered in different ways. Suppose you lived in ancient Rome. You would count the years from the time Rome began as a city. Suppose you lived in ancient Egypt. You would name the years from the time each ruler began to rule.

4   We count years by numbers, too. Sometimes we put the letters B.C. and A.D. after the year. Why do we do this? Do you know what the letters mean? What do we count our years from?

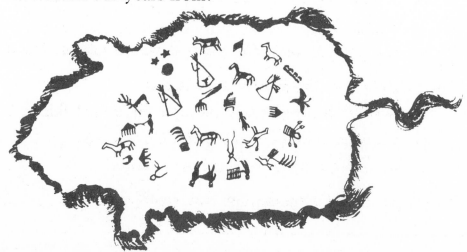

1. The Indians counted years with
   a. pictures.   c. animals.
   b. fire.   d. rivers.

2. The word in the story that means *very old* is _____.

3. The story says, "Indians counted years this way. *They* would draw pictures on animal skins." The word *they* means

   _____ .

4. Which of the following does this story lead you to believe?
   a. Indians had many animals to count.
   b. People in Rome did not know how to count the years.
   c. Keeping count of the years is important to people.

5. How would you count the years if you lived in ancient Rome? (Which sentence is exactly like the one in your book?)
   a. You would count the years from the time Rome began as a city.
   b. You would count the years until you could go to live in Egypt.
   c. You would count the years it would take to leave Rome.

6. The main idea of the whole story is that
   a. Indians drew counting pictures on animal skins.
   b. years have been counted in different ways.
   c. we need kings to tell us how to count.

7. The opposite of *fall* (paragraph two, sentence five) is _____.

The Time of the Falling Leaves

1   How long from one birthday to the next? Very long! In that time, the earth will move all around the sun. How will you know when the year is over? The calendar will tell you.

2   What did people do before there were calendars? They watched the sun, moon, and stars. When they watched the sun, they put cuts in sticks. The cuts marked how many times the sun came up and went down. This was just one way to mark the passing of time.

3   There were other ways. One way was to give time a name. In spring, people said, "It is the time of new leaves." In winter, people said, "It is the time of the great snow."

4   When does your birthday come? In the time of the falling leaves? Or the time of many flowers?

1. The time of the new leaves is
   a. winter.   c. spring.
   b. fall.   d. sun up.

2. The word in the story that means *the time in which the earth moves all around the sun* is _____.

3. The story says, "In spring, people said, 'It is the time of new leaves.'" The word *it* means _____.

4. Which of the following does this story lead you to believe?
   a. There have not always been calendars.
   b. Your birthday is always on January 1st.
   c. We do not need calendars.

5. When did the people put cuts in sticks? (Which sentence is exactly like the one in your book?)
   a. When the new moon came up, they put cuts in sticks.
   b. When they watched the sun, they put cuts in sticks.
   c. They put cuts in sticks when they watched the sun.

6. The main idea of the whole story is that
   a. people liked to watch the sun go up and come down.
   b. people did not want to use calendars.
   c. people used many ways to mark the passing of time.

7. The opposite of *moon* (paragraph two, sentence two) is _____.

Look for a Sign

1   Long ago, people did not know about numerals. When they wanted to know "how many," they put marks in clay. The Egyptians made a line I for each 1. They used the sign Ո for 10. For 100, they used still another sign Ꝯ. Can you tell that this sign Ꝯ Ո ⫴ is 119? Seem funny? But the Egyptians could count many things with these signs.

2   Other early people also made signs for numerals. They made the signs with a pointed stick in the clay. The signs looked like this ▼ ▼ ▼ . For 10, the mark was turned on its side. The Mayans in South America used dots and lines. They made a dot for 1 like this •. They made a line —— for five. Nine looked like this ••••. Ten was 2 lines ====. For 15, they made 3 lines ≡≡≡. This was 19 ≡≡≡.

3   How old are you? Can you write the answer using Egyptian or Mayan signs?

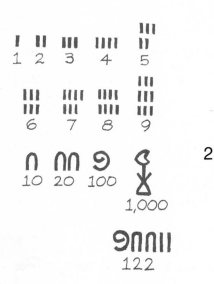

FIND THE ANSWERS

1. Long ago, people did not know about
    a. clay.   c. lines.
    b. numerals.   d. signs.

2. The word in the story that means *lines used for numerals* is

   _____ .

3. The story says, "Other early people also made signs for numerals.
   They made the signs with a pointed stick in the clay." The word

   they means _____ .

4. Which of the following does this story lead you to believe?
    a. It is fun to play with clay.
    b. Pointed sticks were not used to count things.
    c. People long ago made up their own ways to count.

5. How did the Mayans make five? (Which sentence is exactly like
   the one in your book?)
    a. They made a dot · for five.
    b. They made a line ____ for five.
    c. They used sticks made out of clay for five.

6. The main idea of the whole story is that
    a. Egyptians liked to make clay shapes and numbers.
    b. people used different signs for numerals.
    c. people made pointed sticks.

7. The opposite of *young* (paragraph three, sentence one) is

   _____ .

A Leg Walking Right

1   Here are some signs $+ - \div \times$. The signs are very different. They mean very different things. When you see them, you know what to do. This sign $+$ means that you will add some numerals. This sign $-$ means that you will take one numeral away from another. You will subtract. What will you do when you see $\times$ and $\div$?

2   Our signs are easy signs to read. They are easy signs to remember. Look at these two signs ♪⚐. The ancient Egyptians used these signs. A picture of a leg walking to the left ♪ told them to add some numerals. A picture of a leg walking to the right ⚐ told them to subtract.

3   In the 1500s, people used this printed sign & to add numerals. After a while, the sign began to look like this ✦ . Later, the sign became $+$.

4   How much is 2 ♪ 2?

88

1. What do you do when you see this sign **✛** ?
   a. Walk away.   c. Write a numeral.
   b. Read a sign.   d. Add.

2. The word in the story that means *to take one numeral away from another* is _____ .

3. The story says, "Our signs are easy signs to read. *They* are easy signs to remember." The word *they* means _____ .

4. Which of the following does this story lead you to believe?
   a. Egyptians could not add numerals together.
   b. All Egyptians had two left legs.
   c. Our signs are not hard to understand.

5. What did the sign to add numerals begin to look like? (Which sentence is exactly like the one in your book?)
   a. After a while, the sign began to look like this **✦**.
   b. After a while, the sign began to look like this **✛** .
   c. After a while, the sign began to look like this &.

6. The main idea of the whole story is that
   a. the signs for adding and subtracting have changed.
   b. people could not write in the 1500s.
   c. the old signs were good for Egyptians but not for us.

7. The opposite of *right* (paragraph two, sentence five) is _____ .

How the Rabbit Got Its Shape

The children sat down near their grandfather. They wanted a story. "The rabbit is funny," they said. "How did it get that way?"

"Rabbit is funny now," said their grandfather. "But long ago, Rabbit was different. It had a long, bushy tail. It was round and fat. Its legs were straight and strong. It walked and ran the way other animals do." And Grandfather told the children this story.

One day, when Rabbit was in the woods, it met a child. The child's name was Little Fox. Little Fox was crying because she was lost. She could not find her way home.

"Do not cry," Rabbit said. "I will take you home." As they walked through the woods, Little Fox fell into a deep hole. "I will get you out," said Rabbit. It put its long, bushy tail down into the hole. Little Fox pulled on the tail. She pulled so hard Rabbit's tail broke off.

Next, Rabbit put its front legs around a tree. It put its back legs into the hole. Little Fox held on to Rabbit's legs with both hands. She pulled and pulled. Rabbit's legs began to stretch. Its fat body grew thin.

At last, Little Fox was out of the hole. Rabbit and Little Fox walked on through the woods. But now Rabbit could not walk on its long back legs. It had to hop.

At last, they came to the house of Little Fox. Little Fox was happy. But Rabbit was not.

"How can I go home?" Rabbit said. "I look so funny."

"Do not be afraid to go home," said Little Fox. "From now on, all rabbits will look like you."

Grandfather looked at the children. "Now you know," he said, "how rabbits got their shape."

275 words

II

Some Changes Are Fast:
Some Changes Are Slow

In this section you will read about things that change very fast and other things that change very slowly. You will read about changes from the standpoint of history, geography, arithmetic, biology, economics, and anthropology.

Keep these questions in mind when you are reading about these things.

1. Why do some things change fast and others change slowly?

2. What kind of things change slowly?

3. What kind of things change fast?

4. What things can you think of that cause change to happen?

The New Fur Suit

1   Make believe you are an Eskimo. You have a new fur suit. Your family made it for you. The suit has two pair of pants. You wear both pair of pants. The first pair has the fur side inside. The other pair has the fur side outside. The top of the suit has two parts also. You will wear this suit all winter. Boys and girls wear the same kind of clothes.

2   Eskimo children have dressed this way for many years. It is the way their grandparents dressed. Your grandfather may have worn short pants and long stockings as a child. Your grandmother may have had to wear long stockings, too. In the early 1900s, children in our country did not dress like you do. Today, our clothes are very different.

3   Eskimo clothes do not change much. The clothes of some people change all the time.

1. Eskimo children wear
    a. two pair of pants.   c. a long coat.
    b. short stockings.   d. big shoes.

2. The word in the story that means *a set of clothes* is _____ .

3. The story says, "You have a new fur suit. Your family made *it* for you." The word *it* means _____ .

4. Which of the following does this story lead you to believe?
    a. We dress just like the Eskimos.
    b. Eskimos like their grandparents.
    c. Eskimos live in a cold land.

5. How did your grandfather dress? (Which sentence is exactly like the one in your book?)
    a. In the early 1900s, children in our country did not dress like you do.
    b. Your grandfather may have dressed in long stockings.
    c. Your grandfather may have dressed in Eskimo clothes.

6. The main idea of the whole story is that
    a. your grandfather might have been an Eskimo.
    b. Eskimo clothing has not changed.
    c. your grandmother thinks Eskimos are children.

7. The opposite of *summer* (paragraph one, sentence nine) is

    _____ .

Land of the Reindeer

1   The people of Lapland are called Lapps. They came to this cold land of the north thousands of years ago. They lived in tents. They followed the reindeer which moved from place to place looking for food.

2   Today, many Lapps still live in tents. They still follow the reindeer from place to place. These people are the mountain Lapps.

3   But now there are also Lapps who live near rivers and the sea. Most Lapps who live near the sea make their living by fishing. They have small houses made of wood and dirt.

4   Today, many Lapps also live in towns. Some Lapps have farms. They have good houses. They stay in one place.

5   The lives of the Lapps who live by the sea and rivers are changing. These Lapps are changing from old ways to new ways. But the mountain Lapps live the same way as the Lapps of long ago.

1. The Lapps followed
   a. horses.   c. reindeer.
   b. fish.   d. dogs.

2. The word in the story that means *the people who live in Lapland* is _____ .

3. The story says, "Some Lapps have farms. *They* have good houses." The word *they* means _____ .

4. Which of the following does this story lead you to believe?
   a. Lapps do not like to follow reindeer.
   b. All Lapps do not follow the old ways.
   c. The houses in Lapland are all the same.

5. What do the Lapps near the sea have? (Which sentence is exactly like the one in your book?)
   a. They have small houses made like tents.
   b. They have many reindeer as pets.
   c. They have small houses made of wood and dirt.

6. The main idea of the whole story is that
   a. Lapps live in dirty houses.
   b. Lapps live and work in different ways.
   c. the lives of the Lapps are not changing.

7. The opposite of *hot* (paragraph one, sentence two) is

   _____ .

Animal Skin Ball

1   The Indians were making toys for their children. They made a bow and arrow. They put animal skin around a rock and made a ball.

2   Children have played with toys for thousands of years. Once toys were made by hand. They were made from bones or wood or clay. Other things were used, too. People used what they had to make toys. You can still get bows and arrows and balls. But today, these things are made by machines.

3   When toys were made by hand, children did not have many toys. Because they had few toys, children kept them a long time.

4   Have you ever been to a museum? A museum is a building in which old things are kept. Some museums have a room for old toys. Today's toys may be kept in a museum someday.

FIND THE ANSWERS

1. The Indians were making
   a. museums.   c. machines.
   b. toys.   d. houses.

2. The word in the story that means *a building in which old things are kept* is _____.

3. The story says, "The Indians were making toys for their children. *They* made a bow and arrow." The word *they* means

   _____.

4. Which of the following does this story lead you to believe?
   a. Children had to take good care of their toys long ago.
   b. Long ago, children played with old toys in museums.
   c. A rock covered with animal skin makes a good ball.

5. How were toys made long ago? (Which sentence is exactly like the one in your book?)
   a. They were made from bones or wood or clay.
   b. They were made from stones or mud or hay.
   c. They were made by Indians who had children.

6. The main idea of the whole story is that
   a. long ago, toys were made by hand.
   b. today animal skins are kept in museums.
   c. long ago, machines made toys for Indian children.

7. The opposite of *machine* (paragraph two, sentence two) is

   _____.

The School on Wheels

1   Juan was the first to see the bus. He shouted and waved his hands. The other people in the village came running. Everyone shouted and waved. It was the school bus. This bus did not take children to school. In this village in Mexico, there were no schools. The bus was the school! The driver of the bus was the teacher. The bus would stay in the village for three months.

2   In the morning, the teacher gave lessons to the small children. In the afternoon, the big children came. First they worked in the fields. Then they came to school. At night, the men and women went to the school. They wanted to learn, too.

3   Some day the village will have a real school. But now, the school on wheels is the only school the people have. Why do you think these people are so glad to see the school on wheels?

1. When the bus came to the village, the people
   - a. told stories.
   - b. cried and left.
   - c. ran away.
   - d. shouted and waved.

2. The word in the story that means *a small town* is _____.

3. The story says, "Juan was the first to see the bus. *He* shouted and waved his hands." The word *he* means _____ .

4. Which of the following does this story lead you to believe?
   - a. In Mexico, bus drivers are good teachers.
   - b. The people did not want to build a real school.
   - c. The school bus went from one village to another.

5. How long would the bus stay in the village? (Which sentence is exactly like the one in your book?)
   - a. The bus would stay in the fields for many months.
   - b. The bus would stay in the village for three months.
   - c. The bus would stay as long as the people wanted it to stay.

6. The main idea of the whole story is that
   - a. people want to learn to read and write.
   - b. people in Mexico shout a lot.
   - c. small children do not really need lessons.

7. The opposite of *day* (paragraph two, sentence four) is

   _____ .

Signs in the Desert

1   The nomads walked in the desert. It was hot and dry. The people of the tribe needed water. Soon some of the tribe called out. They had seen a few small plants. The plants were a sign. Under the plants they would find a little water. The people began to dig. When they found water, they were very happy. They filled their water bags.

2   Other nomads walked in a desert. They, too, needed water. But they looked for a different sign. They followed a long pipeline. The pipeline carried gas across the desert. The gas company had put in water at some places near the pipeline. These desert people knew they would have water when it was needed.

3   There were signs in the desert for both people. But one followed an old sign. The other followed a new sign.

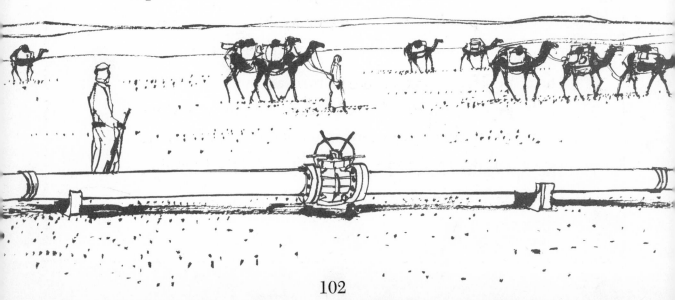

1. The nomads needed
    a. more sun.   c. bags.
    b. water.   d. a pipeline.

2. The word in the story that means *people who travel from place to place looking for food and water* is _____ .

3. The story says, "The nomads walked in the desert. *It* was hot and dry." The word *it* means _____ .

4. Which of the following does this story lead you to believe?
    a. Nomads like to walk in the desert.
    b. Nomads are always happy.
    c. People cannot live without water.

5. What did the pipeline carry? (Which sentence is exactly like the one in your book?)
    a. The pipeline carried the people to the desert.
    b. The pipeline carried water to the gas company.
    c. The pipeline carried gas across the desert.

6. The main idea of the whole story is that
    a. desert people followed different signs to find water.
    b. gas companies put signs on plants in the desert.
    c. the desert people liked to dig up desert plants.

7. The opposite of *lost* (in sentence nine) is _____ .

Kings and Queens of Candy

1   Once candy was not made for children. In one country, almost 5,000 years ago, candy was made only for the rulers. Today, children are the kings and queens of candy.

2   Do you ever eat licorice? People in ancient times ate licorice, too. They did not think of licorice as candy at first. They ate licorice to keep them strong and well. In some countries, people ate licorice to make them beautiful! Later, people ate it just because it tasted good!

3   All candy was made by hand until 1845. In that year, someone made a candy machine. Soon other candy machines were made. At first, not much candy was sold. But by the 1900s, candy was sold all over the world. Today, candy companies say people eat from 15 to 30 pounds of candy a year. More than 2,000 different kinds of candy are made!

4   How many kinds of candy do you eat, your majesty?

104

1. Candy was first made for
   a. children
   b. animals.
   c. rulers.
   d. companies.

2. A word in the story that means *persons who rule over many people* is _____.

3. The story says, "People in ancient times ate licorice, too. *They did not think of licorice as candy at first.*" The word *they* means

   _____.

4. Which of the following does this story lead you to believe?
   a. Today people eat licorice to make their hair grow.
   b. Today people eat licorice because ancient people ate it.
   c. Today people eat licorice because they like it.

5. How many kinds of candy are there? (Which sentence is exactly like the one in your book?)
   a. Not enough kinds of candy are made.
   b. More than 2,000 different kinds of candy are made!
   c. Different kinds of companies make many kinds of candy.

6. The main idea of the whole story is that
   a. candy companies think people eat too much candy.
   b. people have liked candy since ancient times.
   c. licorice will make you grow big and strong.

7. The opposite of *modern* (sentence five) is _____.

The Cat and the Clover

1   A man and woman looked at their field. Once it had been covered with red clover. This plant made good feed for their cows. But now most of the clover was gone. The farmers wanted more red clover in their fields. So they got a cat.

2   The cat hunted for field mice. For years, field mice had been tearing down bumblebee nests. Once bumblebees had carried pollen from one clover to another. Now most of the bumblebees were gone. Without bumblebees to carry the pollen, most of the clover died.

3   The cat killed the mice. Soon there were no mice left. Now other bumblebees began to make new nests. The bumblebees flew over the field. They carried the pollen from clover to clover again.

4   The following year, the man and woman looked at their field. It was covered with red clover. After that, they always kept a cat.

1. The farmers' field had once been covered with
   a. red clover.   c. bumblebees.
   b. field mice.   d. grass.

2. The word in the story that means *the fine yellow dust in the flower of the clover* is _____ .

3. The story says, "The man and woman looked at their field. Once *it* had been covered with red clover." The word *it* means_____ .

4. Which of the following does this story lead you to believe?
   a. Some field mice help farmers to grow better crops.
   b. Some insects and animals are of great help to us.
   c. Cats like to play in clover.

5. What did the cat do? (Which sentence is exactly like the one in your book?)
   a. The cat hunted for bumblebees.
   b. The cat played in the red clover.
   c. The cat hunted for field mice.

6. The main idea of the whole story is that
   a. the cat and the bumblebees helped the farmers.
   b. cats like cows that eat red clover.
   c. bumblebees make honey from red clover only.

7. The opposite of *stopped* (paragraph three, sentence three) is _____ .

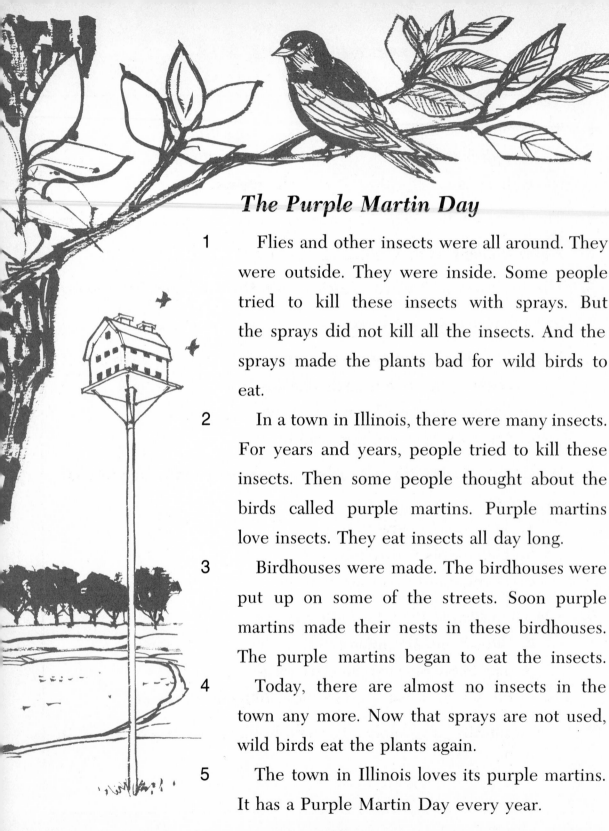

The Purple Martin Day

1   Flies and other insects were all around. They were outside. They were inside. Some people tried to kill these insects with sprays. But the sprays did not kill all the insects. And the sprays made the plants bad for wild birds to eat.

2   In a town in Illinois, there were many insects. For years and years, people tried to kill these insects. Then some people thought about the birds called purple martins. Purple martins love insects. They eat insects all day long.

3   Birdhouses were made. The birdhouses were put up on some of the streets. Soon purple martins made their nests in these birdhouses. The purple martins began to eat the insects.

4   Today, there are almost no insects in the town any more. Now that sprays are not used, wild birds eat the plants again.

5   The town in Illinois loves its purple martins. It has a Purple Martin Day every year.

1. Some people tried to kill
    a. plants.   c. birds.
    b. insects.   d. sprays.

2. The word in the story that means *something made by a bird in which it keeps its eggs* is _____.

3. The story says, "Purple martins love insects. *They* eat insects all day long." The word *they* means _____.

4. Which of the following does this story lead you to believe?
    a. Insect sprays turn birds purple.
    b. Sprays are good for most insects.
    c. Insect sprays can hurt wild birds.

5. What was made? (Which sentence is exactly like the one in your book?)
    a. Birdhouses were made.
    b. Birdhouses were built.
    c. Purple martin houses were made.

6. The main idea of the whole story is that
    a. wild birds eat sprays in Illinois.
    b. purple martins can help us get rid of insects.
    c. in Illinois towns, people have always liked insects.

7. The opposite of *hates* (paragraph five, sentence one) is _____.

Before There Were Birds

1   Insects have lived on earth for millions of years. They lived on earth before there were birds. They lived on earth before there were dinosaurs.

2   Dinosaurs were big animals. One kind of dinosaur was over 70 feet long. Some insects were big, too. The dragonfly was one foot long. Its wings were more than three feet wide. But most insects were small.

3   While the dinosaurs lived, the earth began to change. New mountains pushed up. The weather changed. In some places, there was not much water. Without water, plants could not live. The dinosaurs could not find food or water. The insects did not need much food and water. And they could fly. They could leave one place and fly to another. The dinosaurs died. But the insects lived. They became very small.

4   Today, there are more insects on earth than any other living thing.

110

1. Most insects were
   a. big. c. fat.
   b. small. d. thin.

2. The word in the story that means *go away* is _____.

3. The story says, "But the insects lived. *They* became very small."
   The word *they* means _____.

4. Which of the following does this story lead you to believe?
   a. There was too much water.
   b. Dragonflies became bigger than dinosaurs.
   c. Some animals changed as the earth changed.

5. How could insects find food and water? (Which sentence is exactly like the one in your book?)
   a. They could follow the dinosaurs to find water.
   b. They could eat the dinosaurs' food.
   c. They could leave one place and fly to another.

6. The main idea of the whole story is that
   a. there are no insects today.
   b. dinosaurs did not need much food or water.
   c. insects are the oldest animals on earth.

7. The opposite of *pulled* (paragraph three, sentence two) is

   _____.

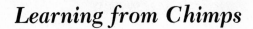

Learning from Chimps

1   Do you think chimpanzees are fun? Many children like the shows at the zoo. The chimps do funny tricks.

2   Jane Goodall wanted to learn about wild chimps and apes. She went to live in a jungle camp to be near the homes of the chimps. The chimps were very shy. They were afraid of people.

3   Jane waited and waited. She waited many months. At last the chimps came close to her. She fed them bananas. The chimps were ready to be friends.

4   The chimps learned to trust Jane. She learned many things about chimps. She learned that they act very much like us. They use parts of trees like tools. They even hug and kiss the way people do.

5   Jane was very happy she had waited so long. She learned that chimps are *very* smart.

1. Chimps in the jungle
       a. love tools.   c. are afraid of people.
       b. hate bananas.   d. like the zoo.

2. The word in the story that means *things that you use to do work*
   is _____.

3. The story says, "At last the chimps came close to her. She fed
   them bananas." The word *them* means _____.

4. Which of the following does this story lead you to believe?
       a. Wild chimps are brave around people.
       b. Wild chimps are fun.
       c. All chimps live in the zoo.

5. Where did Jane go to live in the jungle? (Which sentence is
   exactly like the one in your book?)
       a. She went to live near the zoo.
       b. She went to live in a small town.
       c. She went to live in a jungle camp.

6. The main idea of the whole story is that
       a. sometimes it is good to wait for what we want.
       b. chimps like to wait for people.
       c. people don't like to wait.

7. The opposite of *sad* (paragraph five, sentence one) is

   _____.

Plants That Cure

1   Long ago in Egypt, a queen named Hatshepsut started a search for special plants. She believed that the right plants could help to make sick people well.

2   Today in the jungles there are special hunters. They are not hunting animals. They are looking for plants for medicine.

3   These hunters are scientists. They are men and women who work very hard. They go miles and miles into the jungle rain forest. It is very hot and wet. Many strange plants grow there. Some of the plants grow to giant size.

4   Sometimes very plain plants in the city can help sick people. Even plants like daffodils and buttercups can be used for medicine.

FIND THE ANSWERS

1. The plant hunters are
   a. Egyptian queens.   c. hot and wet.
   b. scientists.   d. sick.

2. The word in the story that means *people who work in and study a science* is _____ .

3. The story says, "These hunters are scientists. *They* are men and women who work very hard." The word *they* means _____ .

4. Which of the following does this story lead you to believe?
   a. Sick people like big plants.
   b. Plants are too hot in the jungle rain forest.
   c. The jungle is a good place for plants to grow.

5. What is it like in the jungle rain forest? (Which sentence is exactly like the one in your book?)
   a. Buttercups grow in the jungle rain forest.
   b. There are many scientists there.
   c. It is very hot and wet.

6. The main idea of the whole story is that
   a. scientists can use plants to make medicines.
   b. eating plants makes you sick.
   c. you should grow your own plants.

7. The opposite of *fancy* (in paragraph four, sentence one) is

   _____ .

Does Your Skin Fit?

1 How does your skin fit? Is it big enough for you? Of course it is. Your skin is the outside covering of your body. It grows with you.

2 Have you ever seen a locust? The covering of this insect does not grow. As the locust gets big, its old skin gets too tight. The locust comes out. It leaves its brown skin behind. The skin looks something like an empty shell.

3 As the locust keeps growing, it keeps changing its skin. The locust changes its skin as much as five times, sometimes more.

4 Like all insects, the locust comes from an egg. Most insects look like worms at first. The locust is different. The young locust never looks like a worm. Right away, it looks like a small locust.

5 Next time you see a shell, look at it carefully. It may be the skin some locust left behind.

FIND THE ANSWERS

1. The covering of a locust
   - a. grows.
   - b. gets too tight.
   - c. is yellow.
   - d. looks like a worm.

2. The word in the story that means *not the same* is

   _____.

3. The story says, "The locust comes out. *It* leaves its brown skin

   behind." The word *it* means _____.

4. Which of the following does this story lead you to believe?
   - a. Each new skin of the locust is larger.
   - b. Locusts do not grow very much in size.
   - c. Big locusts live in empty shells.

5. What does the young locust look like? (Which sentence is exactly like the one in your book?)
   - a. The young locust looks like a shell.
   - b. Right away, it looks like a brown worm.
   - c. Right away, it looks like a small locust.

6. The main idea of the whole story is that
   - a. your skin does not fit you.
   - b. locust shells look like worms.
   - c. the locust changes its skin.

7. The opposite of *full* (paragraph two, sentence six) is _____.

The Fight

1   Do you want to see a fight? Don't move! Look inside you! *I Need* is fighting *I Want*.

2   Your parents give you fifty cents. They want you to buy milk for lunch. You go to the store. Then you see a book you want. Inside you, *I Want* says, "Buy the book." But *I Need* says, "No! You have to get the milk for lunch!" *I Want* is fighting *I Need*.

3   If *I Want* and *I Need* are on the same side, there is no fight. But many times they are on different sides. When this happens, *I Want* often wins the fight.

4   *I Need* does not change much. It always wants the same kinds of things. It wants what you need. *I Want* changes all the time. Today it likes a book. Tomorrow it will be something else.

5   Want to see a fight? Just look inside you!

1. There is a fight going on
   - a. in the street.
   - b. in the air.
   - c. at sea.
   - d. inside you.

2. The word in the story that means *a place where you buy things* is _____ .

3. The story says, "*I Need* does not change much. *It* always wants the same kinds of things." The word *it* means _____ .

4. Which of the following does this story lead you to believe?
   - a. Wants are often stronger than needs.
   - b. Wants do not change very much.
   - c. Some people are always fighting.

5. What happens to *I Need*? (Which sentence is exactly like the one in your book?)
   - a. *I Need* changes a lot.
   - b. *I Need* does not change much.
   - c. *I Want* does not change much.

6. The main idea of the whole story is that
   - a. wants and needs are not always the same.
   - b. it is better to want popcorn than toy cars.
   - c. you must know how to fight to get popcorn.

7. The opposite of *outside* (in sentence three) is _____ .

Bells on Your Ears

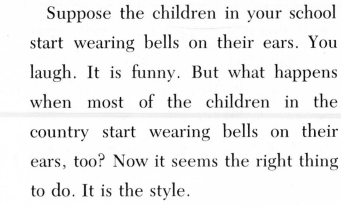

1   Suppose the children in your school start wearing bells on their ears. You laugh. It is funny. But what happens when most of the children in the country start wearing bells on their ears, too? Now it seems the right thing to do. It is the style.

2   In early America, men used to wear wigs. Men in other countries also had wigs. It was the style.

3   People have always tried to color and shape the things around them. This is what we call style.

4   There are styles in many things. There are styles in music. There are styles in gardens. There are styles in painting. Some styles change a little. Some styles change very much. Some styles stay the same.

5   Think of some of the styles we have today. Do you think they will seem funny many years from now?

1. When most of the children in the country wear bells on their ears it is
       a. funny.   c. wrong.
       b. silly.   d. the style.

2. The word in the story that means *coverings of hair to wear over your own hair* is _____.

3. The story says, "Think of some of the styles we have today. Do you think *they* will seem funny many years from now?" The word *they* means _____.

4. Which of the following does this story lead you to believe?
       a. Our styles may seem funny to people from other lands.
       b. We don't know what the style was in early America.
       c. People in other countries should wear wigs today.

5. What did men in early America do? (Which sentence is exactly like the one in your book?)
       a. In early America, the men were in style.
       b. The men wore wigs in early America.
       c. In early America, men used to wear wigs.

6. The main idea of the whole story is that
       a. there are styles in many things.
       b. only men wear wigs.
       c. music is all right for some people.

7. The opposite of *cry* (in sentence two) is _____.

Stone Money, Feather Money

1   I want something you have. You want something I have. Sometimes I give you money. Sometimes you give me money. It can be metal money. It can be paper money.

2   What kind of money did people have long ago? Some people used stones as money. Others used feathers. Many people used animals. Later, gold came into use as money. But this money was hard to carry. It was heavy.

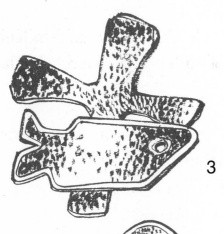

3   Some people thought of making metals in special shapes. Each special shape would be worth something different. In some places, people shaped the gold to look like animals. They still thought of animals as money. Other metals were used, too. The metals could come in any shape. Gold dust was money. Gold bars were money.

4   Today, different countries have different names for money. Sometimes, we call several cents *pennies*. The English call them *pence*. Spanish people call them *centavos* (sen täv′ ōs).

122

1. Long ago, people used as money
       a. paper.   c. animals.
       b. metal.   d. silver.

2. The word in the story that means *something hard to pick up or carry* is _____ .

3. The story says, "In some places, people shaped the gold to look like animals. *They* still thought of animals as money." The word *they* means _____ .

4. Which of the following does this story lead you to believe?
       a. People need money to buy things they want.
       b. Gold is good as money when it is very heavy.
       c. Stones are better than feathers as money.

5. What did the special shapes of the metals mean? (Which sentence is exactly like the one in your book?)
       a. Each special shape would be worth something different.
       b. The people would make metals in special shapes.
       c. Some of the special shapes looked like different animals.

6. The main idea of the whole story is that
       a. animals are too heavy to be used as money.
       b. people make animals out of stone.
       c. people have used different kinds of money.

7. The opposite of *take* (in sentence three) is _____ .

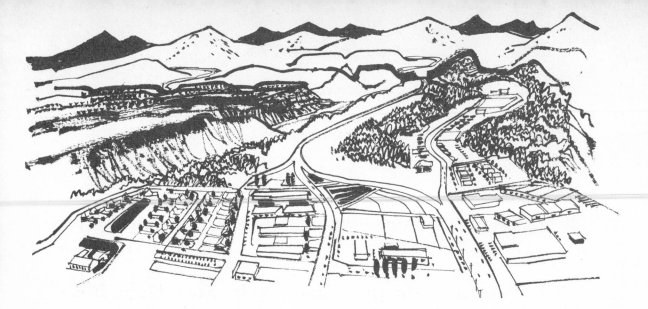

The City That a Secret Built

1   There were a few small houses. There were some stone buildings. These houses and buildings were part of a school. But there was nothing else in this part of the country. It was a good place for secret work. People came to do this secret work in a special kind of building. The secret work was making the atom bomb.

2   Soon many more buildings were needed. By 1960, there were over 300 buildings. The people who worked in these buildings needed houses. Because of this secret work, a city grew very quickly. The city is Los Alamos, New Mexico.

3   It is a different kind of city. People from all over the country can visit Los Alamos. But only people who work in Los Alamos can live there.

4   Los Alamos is a city that a secret built.

1. The houses and buildings were part of a
   a. shopping center.　　　c. city.
   b. school.　　　　　　　d. village.

2. The word in the story that means *something you keep to yourself* is _____ .

3. The story says, "The city is Los Alamos, New Mexico. *It* is a different kind of city." The word *it* means _____ .

4. Which of the following does this story lead you to believe?
   a. Cities are built on secret plans.
   b. Cities grow up near where people work.
   c. The people in Los Alamos had a school.

5. Who can live in Los Alamos? (Which sentence is exactly like the one in your book?)
   a. But only people who work in Los Alamos can live there.
   b. People from all over the country can live in Los Alamos.
   c. People from Mexico can live in Los Alamos.

6. The main idea of the whole story is that
   a. a new school now has 300 buildings.
   b. a new city was built because of secret work.
   c. no one knows there is an atom bomb.

7. The opposite of *same* (paragraph three, sentence one) is

   _____ .

Stop for Fair Rules

1 Once there were no rules to protect workers. Men, women, and even children had to work many hours each day. They were not paid much. Sometimes they got sick. They had to keep working.

2 Then men and women came together to make fair rules for workers. They made good rules. If some workers thought a job was too hard, all the workers could stop working.

3 Sometimes workers stop working when they want more pay. When workers all stop a job together, it is called a "strike."

4 Many years ago, in some Indian tribes, women made the moccasins for the men to wear to war. Sometimes the women leaders in the tribe did not want a war. Then they would stop making moccasins for the men to wear. Were these Indian women going on strike?

FIND THE ANSWERS

1. Once men, women, and children
   - a. got no pay.
   - c. made bad rules.
   - b. were not paid much.
   - d. made moccasins.

2. The word in the story that means *to stop work all together*

   is _____ .

3. The story says, "Men, women, and even children had to work many hours each day. *They* were not paid much." The word

   they means _____ .

4. Which of the following does this story lead you to believe?
   - a. All workers need moccasins.
   - b. Indians liked to strike.
   - c. Once workers did not have fair rules.

5. Why did the Indian women stop making moccasins? (Which sentence is exactly like the one in your book?)
   - a. They wanted to go to war, too.
   - b. They needed more pay for their families.
   - c. Sometimes the women leaders in the tribe did not want a war.

6. The main idea of the whole story is that
   - a. all rules are fair.
   - b. working makes you sick.
   - c. people can make fair rules for themselves.

7. The opposite of *well* (in paragraph one) is _____ .

Old Job or New Job?

1   Some jobs are new. Some jobs are gone. Other jobs are old. We just have new ways of doing them.

2   Long ago, people knew how to make paper by hand. It took a long time for paper to be made this way. After a while, machines were used to make paper. Now people who make paper by hand are not needed any more.

3   Once many people made their own cloth. They got fibers from plants, like flax. They wove the fibers into cloth. They also used plants to make their own dyes for the cloth. Today men and women go to shops to buy many kinds of cloth made by machines.

4   Once people put shoes on horses. Now they put tires on cars.

5   Today, only a few people know how to fly spaceships. Just a few years ago, there were no spaceships. Someday, this may be an old job, too.

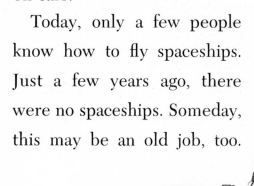

1. Once people put shoes on
   a. cars.   c. their feet.
   b. horses.   d. soldiers.

2. The word in the story that means *something that changes the color of cloth* is _____.

3. The story says, "Once people put shoes on horses. Now *they* put tires on cars." The word *they* means _____.

4. Which of the following does this story lead you to believe?
   a. Paper made by hand is the best paper.
   b. Jobs change as people learn new ways of working.
   c. You have to be old to fly a spaceship.

5. How was paper made long ago? (Which sentence is exactly like the one in your book?)
   a. Long ago, paper was made by hand.
   b. Long ago, people knew how to make paper by hand.
   c. Long ago, some people made paper by machine.

6. The main idea of the whole story is that
   a. there are old jobs and new jobs.
   b. old dye is the best.
   c. we don't need spaceships any more.

7. The opposite of *off* (paragraph four, sentence one) is _____.

The Dog Who Could Not Understand

Once a tiger was in a cage. Soon a good woman went by. As soon as the tiger saw the woman, the tiger began to cry. "Please! Please!" it called. "Please, let me out."

"No," said the good woman. "If I do, you will eat me."

"I will not eat you," the tiger said. "Please let me out."

The good woman believed the tiger. She opened the door of the cage. The tiger jumped out. "How stupid you are," the tiger laughed. "Now I am going to eat you."

"Wait!" the woman cried. "It is wrong to eat me. Let us ask others what they think."

"You may ask three others," the tiger said.

The good woman asked a tree. It said, "I give shade. And yet I am cut down. Let the tiger eat you."

Next, the good woman asked a bird. The bird said, "I hurt no one. Yet people hunt and kill me. Let the tiger eat you."

The last one the good woman asked was the road. The road said, "I don't care if the tiger eats you. People could not get along too well without me. Yet all day long people step on me without even a thank you."

The tiger was ready to eat the good woman. Just then a dog came by. "What is going on?" asked the dog. The woman told the dog the whole story.

"I don't understand," said the dog. "The tiger wants to eat you because you put it in a cage?"

"No, no," said the woman. "Some other people put it in a cage."

"Oh," the dog said. "The tiger is going to eat you because you do not have a cage."

"Stupid dog!" the tiger cried. "Don't you understand? I was in the cage. This woman let me out."

"Oh. I see," the dog said. "When the woman was in the cage, you let her out."

"I was in the cage!" the tiger cried. "Like this!" With that, it jumped back into the cage.

At once, the dog shut the door of the cage. "Oh," the dog laughed. "At last I understand!"

The good woman and the dog walked off. The tiger looked after them.

Then he stretched out in the cage. If he waited long enough, another good person would come by.

Now Reader, try to tell this story to a friend.

The Moving Hill

1   Have you ever seen a hill move? Dunes are sand hills that move. As the wind blows, it moves the sand. It moves the sand against something, like a plant or a rock. The wind moves the sand over and over again. Soon a hill begins to grow. The wind blows more sand to the other side of the hill.

2   Sleeping Bear Dune is a big sand dune near one of the Great Lakes. Many people go to see it. It is hard to walk in the sand. So people ride in special cars. These cars have wide, fat tires. They do not need roads.

3   Sand dunes are found near lakes and oceans. They are also found in the desert. We know hills stay in one place. It may take hundreds of years for the weather to shape hills. Most sand dunes are always moving. The wind makes these moving hills fast.

1. Sand hills are moved by
   a. rocks.   c. wind.
   b. cars.   d. lakes.

2. The word in the story that means *sand hills that move* is

   _____ .

3. The story says, "As the wind blows, *it* moves the sand." The word

   it means the _____ .

4. Which of the following does this story lead you to believe?
   a. The wind blows sand in the ocean.
   b. The wind helps change the land.
   c. Many people live on sand dunes.

5. What is hard to do? (Which sentence is exactly like the one in
   your book?)
   a. It is hard to walk in the sand.
   b. It is hard to move a hill.
   c. It is hard to ride in special cars.

6. The main idea of the whole story is that
   a. cars have flat tires.
   b. sand dunes are always moving.
   c. bears like the Great Lakes.

7. The opposite of *thin* (paragraph two, sentence five) is _____ .

The Day the Houses Fell Down

1   In March 1964, Alaska began to shake. There was a great earthquake. It was the biggest earthquake our country ever had.

2   Stores and houses fell down. One street dropped 30 feet. One island rose 33 feet into the air. Parts of the ocean bottom became dry land. People felt the earthquake hundreds of miles away.

3   Each year there are many earthquakes. Most of them are small. They happen in different parts of the world. We are not sure what makes them. But if you are near, you can see the earth move. You may see a big crack in the ground. Sometimes the land drops on one side of the crack. It goes up on the other side of the crack. There is a new hill. The old world has a new shape.

1. The earthquake in Alaska happened in
   - a. April 1967.
   - b. March 1964.
   - c. June 1864.
   - d. May 1867.

2. The word in the story that means *a strong shaking or moving of the ground* is _____ .

3. The story says, "Each year there are many earthquakes. Most of *them* are small." The word *them* means _____ .

4. Which of the following does this story lead you to believe?
   - a. Earthquakes happen only in Alaska.
   - b. The bottom of the ocean is always dry.
   - c. Earthquakes can do a great deal of harm.

5. Where do earthquakes happen? (Which sentence is exactly like the one in your book?)
   - a. They happen in stores and other buildings.
   - b. They happen in different parts of the world.
   - c. They happen only in small countries.

6. The main idea of the whole story is that
   - a. earthquakes change the land.
   - b. houses fall down and streets are broken.
   - c. Alaska shakes a lot.

7. The opposite of *far* (paragraph three, sentence five) is

   _____ .

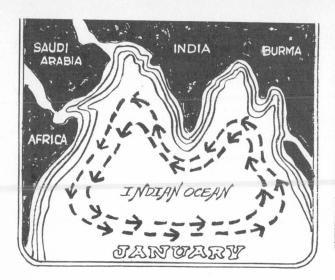 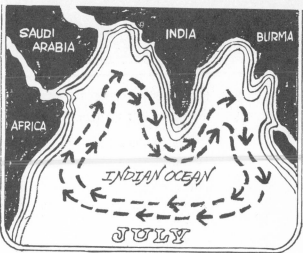

The River in the Ocean

1   The water races. It moves like a fast river. It is called a current. A current is water moving one way. Far from our country, there is a current that moves like a river. This river races faster than any other current in the world. It is in the Indian Ocean.

2   This current is pushed by strong winds. These winds are called monsoon (mon sün′) winds. All summer, the monsoon winds push the current north. The monsoon winds bring heavy rains to many countries.

3   In fall, something happens. The river in the ocean does not race any more. It becomes a slow moving current. After a while, the current stops. But now the monsoon winds begin to blow again. They blow the other way! Now they push the current south.

4   No other river races, slows down, stops, and then goes back the other way.

FIND THE ANSWERS

1. The current moves like a fast
   a. ocean.   c. river.
   b. wind.   d. Indian.

2. The word in the story that means *water moving one way* is

   _____ .

3. The story says, "The water races. *It* moves like a fast river."

   The word *it* means _____ .

4. Which of the following does this story lead you to believe?
   a. All currents are the same.
   b. Winds help make currents.
   c. Indians like the ocean.

5. What do the monsoon winds bring? (Which sentence is exactly
   like the one in your book?)
   a. The monsoon winds bring Indians to the ocean.
   b. The monsoon winds bring heavy snows to many countries.
   c. The monsoon winds bring heavy rains to many countries.

6. The main idea of the whole story is that
   a. the monsoon winds always blow the same way.
   b. the Indian Ocean has a different kind of current.
   c. winds in summer are stronger than winds in winter.

7. The opposite of *goes* (last sentence) is _____ .

Hurakan, God of the Big Wind

1   Far out at sea, the wind is blowing. It blows the water into waves. The waves move toward the land. Wave after wave rolls up on the sand. Each wave brings in some sand. It washes up seashells and pieces of wood. Then the water runs back into the sea. It takes sand back with it. When the wind blows hard, the waves are high. They roll up farther on the shore.

2   Every wave changes the shore. The shoreline looks a little different each day. But it is hard to see the change.

3   Very strong winds are called hurricanes. Hurricanes blow down trees and houses. Big waves beat against the shore. In a few hours, the shoreline looks different. It is easy to see the change.

4   Hurricanes are named after Hurakan (hü rə kän′), the West Indian god of the big wind. The hurricane has a good name. It means "to blow away."

140

1. The wind blows the water into
   - a. pieces of wood.
   - b. hills.
   - c. rain.
   - d. waves.

2. The word in the story that means *some very strong winds* is

   _____ .

3. The story says, "Far out at sea, the wind is blowing. *It* blows the water into waves." The word *it* means the _____ .

4. Which of the following does this story lead you to believe?
   - a. Hurricanes are good.
   - b. Hurricanes can hurt people.
   - c. Hurricanes are named after waves.

5. What do waves do to the shore? (Which sentence is exactly like the one in your book?)
   - a. Every wave blows down a tree.
   - b. Every wave changes the shore.
   - c. Every wave has a name.

6. The main idea of the whole story is that
   - a. hurricanes make fast changes in the land.
   - b. waves bring seashells in to shore.
   - c. the West Indians like the wild hurricanes.

7. The opposite of *easy* (paragraph two, sentence three) is

   _____ .

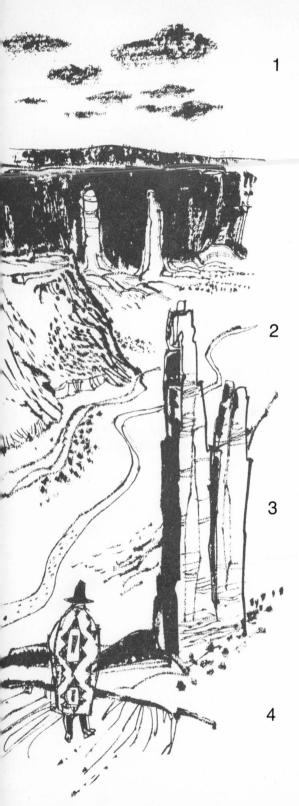

Shapes from the Past

1   The Indians looked down at the rocks. The rocks had different colors. They had many different shapes. The Indians gave the rocks a name. The Indians called them "red rocks standing like people." The rocks had not always looked like standing people. Over a long time, the weather had given these rocks their strange shapes.

2   Weather wears away all rocks. Wind and water turn some rocks into sand and dust. The sand and dust blow away. They become part of the earth. Other rocks, like the red rocks, are changed into strange shapes as they wear away.

3   Wind and rain wear down the soft rocks first. Hard rocks last a long time. In the desert, wind and sand shape the rocks. Some hard rocks look like bridges. Some look like castles. Some rocks look like chimneys without houses. They are called chimney rocks.

4   Someday, all these rocks will have other shapes.

FIND THE ANSWERS

1. The rocks were changed by
   a. the weather.   c. the trees.
   b. the Indians.   d. strange people.

2. The word in the story that means *the form of things* is

   _____ .

3. The story says, "The rocks had different colors. *They* had many

   different shapes." The word *they* means _____ .

4. Which of the following does this story lead you to believe?
   a. Soft rocks make good bridges.
   b. The land will look different someday.
   c. Indians think rocks are people.

5. What does weather do to rocks? (Which sentence is exactly like
   the one in your book?)
   a. Weather turns sand into red rocks.
   b. Weather wears away all rocks.
   c. Weather makes Indians call rocks names.

6. The main idea of the whole story is that
   a. Indians named rocks.
   b. rocks become chimneys.
   c. weather changes rocks.

7. The opposite of *all* (paragraph two, sentence four) is _____ .

Rivers at Work

1   The Colorado and the Mississippi are both rivers. They have been working for millions of years. The fast, young Colorado helped make the Grand Canyon. It has cut away more than 5,000 feet of rock. In the same time, the Mississippi has been working, too. It made a wide valley. But it washed away only 150 feet of rock.

2   The Mississippi is an old river. Old rivers are slow moving. Old rivers are wide. When heavy rains fall, the rivers become even wider. They carry dirt and mud to the ocean. It takes old rivers a long time to change the land.

3   The Colorado is a young river. Young rivers are not wide. The water races along. Sometimes the water falls over rocks high in the air. Sometimes pieces of stone break off. It does not take a young river long to change the land.

1. The Mississippi River made
   - a. a wide canyon.
   - b. a wide valley.
   - c. a deep waterfall.
   - d. a young river.

2. The word in the story that means *moving very fast* is _____.

3. The story says, "When heavy rains fall, the rivers become even wider. *They* carry dirt and mud to the ocean." The word *they* means _____.

4. Which of the following does this story lead you to believe?
   - a. The land changed more in some places than in other places.
   - b. Only slow rivers can change the land.
   - c. Rivers have to be wide and deep in order to change the land.

5. What do we know about the Colorado River? (Which sentence is exactly like the one in your book?)
   - a. The fast, young Colorado cut away many feet of hard rock.
   - b. The fast, young Colorado helped make the Grand Canyon.
   - c. The young Colorado River is wide and fast.

6. The main idea of the whole story is that
   - a. rivers change the land.
   - b. rivers are full of mud.
   - c. water can fall over rocks.

7. The opposite of *climbs* (in paragraph three, sentence four) is _____.

Ghost Town

1   The wind blows down the empty street. There are no cars or people on the street. Grass and weeds grow there. The wind blows through houses. The boards shake. No one cares. The houses are gray and empty. This is a ghost town.

2   Most ghost towns are in the mountains. They were built near old mines. Men came to work in the mines. They were looking for gold and silver.

3   Men and women came with their families. They built houses. Soon there were stores selling food and other things. There were many shops. The town was a busy place.

4   In twenty years, the gold and silver were gone. The families left. The people who owned the shops left. All the people moved on. Today, only empty, old buildings are there. Can you tell why it is called a ghost town?

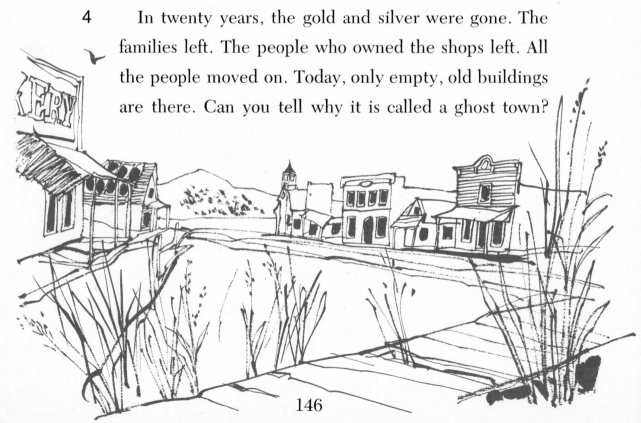

FIND THE ANSWERS

1. When the gold and silver were gone, the people
   a. cried.   c. sang.
   b. left.   d. stayed.

2. The words in the story that mean *a place no one lives in any more*

   are _____ .

3. The story says, "Men and women came with their families. *They*

   built houses." The word *they* means _____ .

4. Which of the following does this story lead you to believe?
   a. Many families live in ghost towns.
   b. People make a town live and grow.
   c. Most towns are gray and empty.

5. Where are most of the ghost towns? (Which sentence is exactly
   like the one in your book?)
   a. Most ghost towns are in South America.
   b. Most ghost towns are in the mountains.
   c. Most ghost towns are busy places.

6. The main idea of the whole story is that
   a. some towns that were once busy became ghost towns.
   b. houses and stores are built in mines.
   c. gold is very difficult to find in a busy old town.

7. The opposite of *came* (in paragraph four, sentence two) is

   _____ .

The Pike Across the Road

1   The roads of England were bad. It was hard to go from town to town. In the spring, the mud was deep. Horses fell into holes. Wheels got stuck in the mud. People could not walk on the roads. They had to walk through fields and woods. The soldiers could not march.

2   In 1751, England began to build new roads. The new roads could be used all year long. People and goods could move from town to town.

3   People had to pay to use the new roads. Gates were put up. A long pole called a pike was placed across the road. People gave money to the gatekeeper. Then the gatekeeper turned the pike out of the way. The roads were called turnpikes.

4   The word *turnpike* is still used today. Our wide turnpikes go all across the land. They make it easy for people to go from place to place.

1. The mud was deep on the roads in the
   a. summer.   c. winter.
   f. fall.   d. spring.

2. The word in the story that means *a long pole placed across a road* is _____ .

3. The story says, "People could not walk on the roads. *They* had to walk through fields and woods." The word *they* means

   _____ .

4. Which of the following does this story lead you to believe?
   a. No one liked the new roads.
   b. People like to pay money to the gatekeeper.
   c. Traveling on turnpikes is faster than on old roads.

5. What did the people do when they couldn't walk on the roads? (Which sentence is exactly like the one in your book?)
   a. They had to walk through fields and woods.
   b. They had to walk through the towns.
   c. They had to march with the soldiers.

6. The main idea of the whole story is that
   a. England is full of mud.
   b. people need good roads.
   c. soldiers can't march.

7. The opposite of *good* (in sentence one) is _____ .

The Peach Basket Game

1   Basketball is an American game. A man named James Naismith made it up in 1891. He wanted a game to play inside in the winter. The first real game was played in 1892.

2   Naismith put up two peach baskets. There were nine players on each side. The players tried to throw the ball into the baskets. There were no holes in the bottom of the baskets. When a ball went into the basket, it stayed there. The game had to stop. A player climbed up to get the ball. It was a slow game. After a while, net baskets were used. The bottoms were cut out of the baskets.

3   At first, many persons could play. Now only ten team members play the game. There are five players on each side. Basketball today is a very fast game.

4   Once basketball was played only in this country. Now basketball is played in many lands.

1. James Naismith wanted a game to play in the
   a. spring.   c. fall.
   b. winter.   d. summer.

2. The word in the story that means *something you play for fun*

   is _____ .

3. The story says, "When a ball went into the basket, *it* stayed

   there." The word *it* means _____ .

4. Which of the following does this story lead you to believe?
   a. We still use peach baskets when we play this game.
   b. A good game does not always have to be a new game.
   c. Basketball began as a farmer's game.

5. What happened when the ball went into the peach basket?
   (Which sentence is exactly like the one in your book?)
   a. When a ball went in the basket, they called Mr. Naismith.
   b. When a ball went in the basket, the bottoms were cut out.
   c. When a ball went in the basket, it stayed there.

6. The main idea of the whole story is that
   a. peaches are good to eat.
   b. most games are not much fun.
   c. basketball is a good game.

7. The opposite of *tops* (paragraph two, sentence four) is

   _____ .

Whales in Trouble

1   Some people in small boats are hunting a whale. When they are near the whale, they throw harpoons. Harpoons are like long, pointed sticks.

2   The hunters pull the whale to land. They cut up the meat and cook it. These people hunt whales just as they did a hundred years ago.

3   Once American whaling ships sailed across the sea. It took them three to five years to bring back a whale.

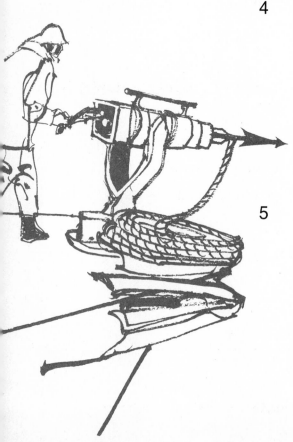

4   Today, it takes only a few days to get a whale. Fliers in an airplane look for whales. When they see one, they call a whaling ship. The whale hunters go out in fast boats. They fire harpoons at the whale. The harpoons have small bombs in them. They kill the whale.

5   The hunt is not fair anymore. Whales cannot fight back. People are being careless about other forms of life on earth. Someday there may be no whales left to hunt!

1. People in small boats hunted whales with
   - a. rocks.
   - b. machines.
   - c. cooks.
   - d. harpoons.

2. The word in the story that means *something like a long, pointed stick* is _____.

3. The story says, "The hunters pull the whale to land. *They* cut up the meat and cook it." The word *they* means _____.

4. Which of the following does this story lead you to believe?
   - a. Whales like hunters in small boats.
   - b. Ways of doing things change.
   - c. Whales are 100 years old.

5. How long does it take to get a whale today? (Which sentence is exactly like the one in your book?)
   - a. Today, it takes only a few days to get a whale.
   - b. Today, it takes many months to catch a whale.
   - c. Today, whales are hunted by airplanes in a few days.

6. The main idea of the whole story is that
   - a. hunters throw harpoons at whaling ships.
   - b. airplanes are good for whales.
   - c. hunting whales today is fast.

7. The opposite of *big* (sentence one) is _____.

The Big Dogs

1   The Sioux Indians lived near the plains. They hunted buffalo. But they did not go far. They had no horses. They lived this way for many years.

2   There were no horses in this country until 1519. Then soldiers and explorers came from Spain. They brought horses with them. Some of the horses were lost. They became wild.

3   About 1600, the Sioux Indians found some of the wild horses. They thought the horses were big dogs. The Indians soon learned how wonderful the "big dogs" were. On horses, the Sioux could follow the buffalo for many miles. Now the Sioux did not have to stay in one place.

4   Soon the Sioux became a strong people. They took what they wanted from other Indians. The other Indians could not catch them. But before long, other Indians had horses, too.

5   Once Indians had horses, their lives changed quickly in many ways.

154

1. Horses were brought from
    - a. the plains.
    - b. Mexico.
    - c. Spain.
    - d. the hills.

2. The word in the story that means *big open fields* or *flat country* is

    _____ .

3. The story says, "Some of the horses were lost. *They* became wild."

    The word *they* means _____ .

4. Which of the following does this story lead you to believe?
    - a. The wild horse has always lived in North America.
    - b. Horses made an Indian nation strong.
    - c. Indians hunted horses for food.

5. What did the Sioux do when they became strong? (Which sentence is exactly like the one in your book?)
    - a. They took what they wanted from other Indians.
    - b. They took all the Indians they wanted.
    - c. They turned their big dogs into horses to ride.

6. The main idea of the whole story is that
    - a. explorers and soldiers are wild men from Spain.
    - b. the horse changed the lives of the Indians.
    - c. strong people who have horses become Indians.

7. The opposite of *go* (paragraph three, sentence five) is _____ .

Books in Chains

1   Have you ever seen a book in chains? Long ago, very few people could read. They did not have books at home. Books were kept in special libraries. Sometimes the books were chained to tables.

2   In those days, people had to write all books by hand. They painted beautiful pictures in many of the books. Only one book could be made at a time. Making a book was very slow work. Sometimes it took years just to make one book.

3   Later, printing machines were made. Machines could print many books at one time. Soon people began to learn to read. They wanted more books. Better printing machines were made to give the people more books. Now printing machines run day and night. They print thousands of books in just a few days.

4   How many different books do you use in school today?

1. Long ago, very few people could
   a. read.   c. laugh.
   b. dance.   d. jump.

2. The word in the story that means *something not like other things* is _____ .

3. The story says, "Soon people began to learn to read. *They* wanted more books." The word *they* means _____ .

4. Which of the following does this story lead you to believe?
   a. Books are important to people.
   b. Books must have chains.
   c. It is not good to put pictures in books.

5. What happened when people began to learn to read? (Which sentence is exactly like the one in your book?)
   a. They wanted more printing machines.
   b. They wanted more books.
   c. They wanted more teachers.

6. The main idea of the whole story is that
   a. machines cannot print books with many pictures in them.
   b. making books with printing machines takes a long time.
   c. printing machines made it easy for people to get books.

7. The opposite of *night* (paragraph three, sentence six) is

   _____ .

Sixteen Left Feet

1   We measure things in feet. We measure things in yards. We also measure things in rods. One rod is the same as $5\frac{1}{2}$ yards. It is the same as $16\frac{1}{2}$ feet.

2   Once the rod was called a "rood." Land was measured in roods. People did not know just how long a rood was. How do you think they found out?

3   One way was to stop sixteen people as they came out of church. The people could be tall. The people could be short. But there had to be sixteen in all. Each one had to put the left foot out. Each left foot had to be behind another left foot. Sixteen left feet made one rood.

4   Now you know how we got the word "rod." Can you find out how we got the words "feet" and "yard"?

one rod

1. Sixteen people were stopped as they came out of
    a. the store.   c. the sky.
    b. the ground.   d. the church.

2. The word in the story that means *a building where people go to pray* is _____ .

3. The story says, "One rod is the same as $5\frac{1}{2}$ yards. *It* is the same as $16\frac{1}{2}$ feet." The word *it* means _____ .

4. Which of the following does this story lead you to believe?
    a. Measuring sixteen left feet was a poor way to measure.
    b. Only sixteen people went to church on the same day.
    c. Only the feet of tall people could be measured easily.

5. What did the people do? (Which sentence is exactly like the one in your book?)
    a. Each one tried to grow very tall.
    b. Each one had to put the left foot out.
    c. Each one took off the left shoe at church.

6. The main idea of the whole story is that
    a. only left feet were used in measuring roods.
    b. people once used rods and roods to measure things.
    c. short people are better than tall people for measuring.

7. The opposite of *short* (paragraph three, sentence two) is

_____ .

Make a Fist

1   "Make a fist," Mary Brown said. The boy made a fist. Mary Brown took the heel and toe of the sock. She tried to make them meet around the fist. If the heel and toe met around the fist, the sock would fit the boy. This was how she measured size.

2   Bob Smith needed three yards of cloth. He put one part of the cloth against his nose. He held the rest of the cloth out as far as his arm could go. "One yard," Bob Smith said. He did this three times. He now had three yards of cloth. This was how he measured cloth. Your grandparents may have measured things this way.

3   Today, we do not have to make a fist to get the right size for socks. We do not have to put cloth against our noses to measure it. How do we measure? Do we guess, or do we know?

1. The boy made a fist to
   - a. start a fight with someone.
   - c. stand on his head.
   - b. see if the sock would fit.
   - d. eat a sock.

2. The word in the story that means *a hand closed up tight* is
   _____ .

3. The story says, "Bob Smith needed three yards of cloth. *He* put one part of the cloth against his nose." The word *he* means
   _____ .

4. Which of the following does this story lead you to believe?
   - a. We have better ways to measure cloth today.
   - b. Bob Smith had a big nose and long arms.
   - c. Bob Smith needed to measure many yards of cloth.

5. What did Mary Brown try to do? (Which sentence is exactly like the one in your book?)
   - a. She tried to start a fight with the boy.
   - b. She tried to measure the cloth with her nose.
   - c. She tried to make them meet around the fist.

6. The main idea of the whole story is that
   - a. Bob Smith was a very clever man who invented measures.
   - b. cloth cannot be measured by using your arms.
   - c. people used their fists and arms to measure things.

7. The opposite of *toe* (in sentence three) is _____ .

Something for Nothing

1   Once there was no zero. To write numerals for sixty-three, people wrote 63. To write six hundred three, people wrote 6 3. The space was there to mean "not any" tens. Sometimes people did not remember the space. It was hard to see and to read.

2   Later, people used a dot to hold the space. Six hundred three looked like this 6.3. But the dot was hard to see. So people put a circle around it like this 6⊙3. Then people could see the dot. They remembered the space.

3   At last, only the circle around the dot was used. It was like a zero. This is one story of how the zero came to be used.

4   Now zero has many important uses. Zero tells how many. Can you tell some other ways zero is used?

FIND THE ANSWERS

1. Sometimes people did not remember
       a. to read.   c. a story.
       b. to eat.   d. a space.

2. The word in the story that means *a circle that means "not any"* is _____ .

3. The story says, "Then the people could see the dot. *They* remembered the space." The word *they* means _____ .

4. Which of the following does this story lead you to believe?
       a. People long ago didn't know how to make dots.
       b. We cannot count without the zero.
       c. People like to tell stories about the zero.

5. What was the space there for? (Which sentence is exactly like the one in your book?)
       a. The space was there to make room for people.
       b. The space was there to mean "not any" tens.
       c. The space was there to make reading hard.

6. The main idea of the whole story is that
       a. the zero is important.
       b. dots look pretty in circles.
       c. you must never use a zero.

7. The opposite of *forget* (in sentence five) is _____ .

The Machine That Knows the Answers

1   There are all kinds of machines. They are used in many different ways. One kind of machine is called a computer (kəm pūt´ėr). A computer can do many things. A computer can do arithmetic. People can do arithmetic. But they cannot do it as fast as a computer.

2   Computers remember things. Computers remember everything people tell them. People cannot remember as many things as computers. Computers help tell what the weather will be. Computers help fly rockets and spaceships.

3   These are only some of the ways computers are used. They are used in thousands of places. But they are not always used the same way. Some computers do just a few things. Some computers can do many things. There are small computers. There are big computers.

4   There may be computers in your school. Can you find out what they do?

1. A computer is a kind of
      a. toy.   c. machine.
      b. animal.   d. person.

2. The word in the story that means *machines that remember things*
   is _____ .

3. The story says, "There are all kinds of machines. *They* are used
   in many different ways." The word *they* means _____ .

4. Which of the following does this story lead you to believe?
      a. Computers make people do their own arithmetic.
      b. People can work better and faster with computers.
      c. All computers are very big and very, very noisy.

5. What do computers remember? (Which sentence is exactly like
   the one in your book?)
      a. Computers remember everything people tell them.
      b. Computers remember what you do in school.
      c. Computers remember what other computers have done.

6. The main idea of the whole story is that
      a. everybody likes to do arithmetic.
      b. your school is a spaceship.
      c. computers can do many things.

7. The opposite of *nothing* (paragraph two, sentence two) is

   _____ .

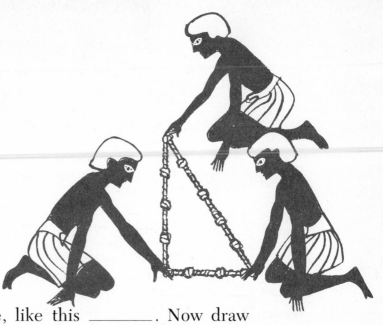

The Rope Stretchers

1   Draw a straight line, like this _____. Now draw another line, like this ⌐____. Do you know what we call this? A right angle.

2   Long ago, in Egypt, right angles were used to measure land. People who did this work were called "rope stretchers." They used long, heavy ropes. Each rope had 12 knots. The space between the knots was always the same.

3   It took three people to make a right angle. One person held both ends of the rope. The second person counted 3 knots from one end of the rope. The next person counted 4 knots from the other end of the rope. Then they pulled the rope tight. The "rope stretchers" had made a right angle.

4   We still measure land. But our way of measuring is different. We do not use ropes. We use special tools. Have you ever seen people using these special tools?

1. Long ago, in Egypt, right angles were used to
    a. measure land.   c. give three people jobs.
    b. stretch rope.   d. make ropes heavy.

2. The word in the story that means *ropes or strings tied together*
    is _____.

3. The story says, "People who did this work were called "rope
    stretchers." *They* used long, heavy ropes." The word *they*
    means _____.

4. Which of the following does this story lead you to believe?
    a. People never used right angles to measure land in Egypt.
    b. No one can draw a really straight line.
    c. It was not easy work to measure the land.

5. How many people did it take to make a right angle? (Which
    sentence is exactly like the one in your book?)
    a. It took four people to make a right angle.
    b. It took three people to make a right angle.
    c. It took twelve people to make a right angle.

6. The main idea of the whole story is that
    a. people in Egypt had a lot of ropes.
    b. people in Egypt carried ropes on stretchers.
    c. rope stretchers measured the land in Egypt.

7. The opposite of *loose* (paragraph three, sentence five) is

    _____.

A Dusty Way to Count

1   Have you ever seen an abacus (ab′ə kəs)? An abacus has rows of beads on wires. The beads are called counters. The counters can be moved up and down on the wires. People in ancient times used the abacus. Some people in Asia still use it. But in most places new ways of counting are used.

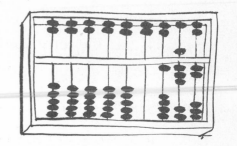

2   In ancient times, an abacus was made in the dust or sand. People would draw lines in the dust for ones, for tens, for hundreds, for thousands. Stones were put on the lines. The stones were used as counters.

3   Later, sticks were used as lines. Stones with holes were put on the sticks.

4   Some people used the tops of tables as an abacus. They would draw lines on the table. They used pebbles as counters. Our word "counter" comes from this way of counting.

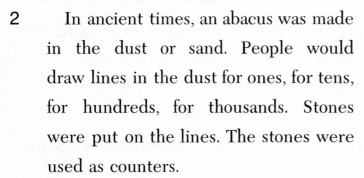

168

FIND THE ANSWERS

1. On an abacus, the counters are
   a. bones.   c. sticks.
   b. beads.   d. wires.

2. The word in the story that means *small stones* is _____.

3. The story says, "People in ancient times used the abacus. Some people in Asia still use *it*." The word *it* means _____.

4. Which of the following does this story lead you to believe?
   a. Ancient people liked beads and stones with holes.
   b. People in Asia did not need to count things.
   c. It was not easy to use an abacus made in dust.

5. What was put on the lines in the dust? (Which sentence is exactly like the one in your book?)
   a. Beads were put on the lines.
   b. Sticks were put on the lines.
   c. Stones were put on the lines.

6. The main idea of the whole story is that
   a. beads look good on wires or on sticks.
   b. the best way to count is with beads or stones.
   c. ancient people used the abacus for counting.

7. The opposite of *goes* (paragraph four, sentence four) is

_____.

Fill in your record chart after each test. Beside the page numbers, put a one for each correct question. Put zero in the box of each question you missed. At the far right, put your total. Seven is a perfect score for each test.

When you finish all the tests in a concept, total your scores by question. Thirty-six is the highest possible score for each question.

When you have taken several tests, check to see which questions you get right each time. Which ones are you missing? Find the places where you need help. For example, if you are missing Question 3 often, ask for help in learning to use directing words.

As you begin each concept, copy the chart onto lined paper. Down the left side are the test page numbers. Across the top are the question numbers and the kinds of questions. For example, each Question 1 in this book asks you to recall a fact. Your scores for each question show how well you are learning each skill.

Your Reading Scores

Concept I

	Question 1 fact	Question 2 vocabulary	Question 3 antecedent	Question 4 inference	Question 5 confirming content	Question 6 main idea	Question 7 vocabulary-opposites	Total for Page
Page 15								
17								
19								
21								
23								
25								
27								
29								
31								
33								
35								
37								
39								
41								
43								
45								
47								
49								
55								
57								
59								
61								
63								
65								
67								
69								
71								
73								
75								
77								
79								
81								
83								
85								
87								
89								
Totals by question								

Your Reading Scores
Concept II

	Question 1 fact	Question 2 vocabulary	Question 3 antecedent	Question 4 inference	Question 5 confirming content	Question 6 main idea	Question 7 vocabulary-opposites	Total for Page
Page 95								
97								
99								
101								
103								
105								
107								
109								
111								
113								
115								
117								
119								
121								
123								
125								
127								
129								
135								
137								
139								
141								
143								
145								
147								
149								
151								
153								
155								
157								
159								
161								
163								
165								
167								
169								
Totals by question								

WORDS YOU WILL NEED

These are words and names that are hard to read. Learn how to say each word. Find the word in the story. Learn the meaning. Use the word in a sentence of your own.

P. 14
cards
Earl of Sandwich
sandwich
wonderful

P. 16
masks
medicine men
medicine women
totem poles

P. 18
collectors
scientists
tools
trash
treasures

P. 20
cables
key
kite
kites
lightning
wire

P. 22
adobe
apartment
bricks
ladders
pueblo

P. 24
airplanes
breathe

dizzy
higher
lungs
oxygen
pilots
South America
tank
thinner

P. 26
acorn
dug
shoot

P. 28
ancestor
hunters
jobs
tame

P. 30
forest
hoof
millions
running

P. 32
hummingbird
liquid
nectar
peas
smallest

P. 34
forest
giant
lightning

rotted
rotting

P. 36
pads
snore
sticky
whistles

P. 38
tools
useful

P. 40
liquid
machine
marbles
threads

P. 42
Egypt
Eugenie Clark
ocean
poison
Red Sea
scientist
sharks
sole
someday

P. 44
ads
advertising
criers
later
newspapers
printing

P. 46
cannot
cereal
important
vote

P. 48
beavers
explore
fancy
France
fur
furs
traders
wonderful

P. 50–53
oldest
redbud

P. 54
melts
snakes

P. 56
dirt
fossil
leaf
million
scientists

P. 58
mountaintops

P. 60
Canada
dirt

glacier
inches
melt
million

P. 62
Colorado
digging
dirt
Grand Canyon
layers
millions
mules

P. 64
cone
lava
melted
Mexico
Parícutin
volcano
volcanoes

P. 66
factories
villages

P. 68
aren't
coughing
dishcloth
pepper
string
tooth
warts

P. 70
language
Latin
pupils
Romans
Rome

P. 72
America
cinnamon
pepper
spices

P. 74
armies
drum
later
message
pigeons
runner
village

P. 76
benches
berries
desks
dunce
ink
odd
pioneer
slates

P. 78
curved
tracks

P. 80
exactly
hunter
knot
numerals
pile

P. 82
Egypt
Rome
rule
ruler

P. 84
calendar

P. 86
clay
dots
Egyptians
Mayans
numerals
South America

P. 88
add
ancient
Egyptians
later
numerals
printed
subtract

P. 90–92
bushy
hop
stretch

P. 94
Eskimo
fur
grandparents
pants
stockings

P. 96
dirt
Lapland
Lapps
reindeer

P. 98
clay
machines
museum

P. 100
driver
everyone
Juan
Mexico
running
shouted
village

P. 102
desert
gas
nomads
pipeline
tribe

P. 104
ancient
later
licorice
machine
majesty

P. 106
bumblebee
clover
pollen

P. 108
birdhouses
Illinois
insects
purple martins
sprays

P. 110
dinosaurs
dragonfly
insects
millions

P. 112
apes
bananas
chimpanzees
chimps
Jane Goodall
hug
jungle
kiss
shy
trust
wild

P. 114
buttercups
daffodils
Egypt
Hatshepsut
hunters
hunting
jungles
medicine
plain
scientists
search

P. 116
carefully
empty
insects
locust
tight

P. 118
fifty

P. 120
America
style
wigs

P. 122
bars

centavos
English
later
metal
pence
Spanish
special
worth

P. 124
atom bomb
Los Alamos
New Mexico
quickly
secret
special

P. 126
Indian
leaders
mocassins
tribe

P. 128
dyes
fibers
flax
jobs
machines
spaceships
wove

P. 130–133
shade
stretched
stupid
understand

P. 134
desert
dune
Great Lakes

Sleeping Bear Dune
special

P. 136
Alaska
biggest
crack
earthquake
island

P. 138
current
faster
Indian Ocean
monsoon

P. 140
farther
Hurakan
hurricanes
seashells
shore
shoreline
toward
West Indian

P. 142
castles
chimneys
desert
strange

P. 144
Colorado
dirt
Grand Canyon
millions
Mississippi
wider

P. 146
empty
ghost

P. 148
gatekeeper
pike
pole
stuck
turnpikes

P. 150
basketball
James Naismith
net
peach

P. 152
bombs
harpoons
hunters
machines
whale
whaling

P. 154
buffalo
explorers
quickly
Sioux
Spain
wonderful

P. 156
chains
later
libraries
machines
printing
special

P. 158
rods
rood
sixteen

P. 160
fist
grandparents
heel
sock

P. 162
dot
later

numerals
zero

P. 164
arithmetic
cannot
computer
machines
rockets
spaceships

P. 166
angle
Egypt
knots
special
stretchers
tight
tools

P. 168
abacus
ancient
Asia
beads
counters
later
pebbles
wires

6 7 8 9 10   VHVH   86 85 84 83 82 81